… a profound grasp of the Industry.

Ron Peltier
CEO, Home Services of America

… the industry's premier Report.

Lennox Scott
CEO, John L. Scott Real Estate

One of the best jobs of 'Pulling It All Together' that I have seen.

Dale Stinton
CEO, National Association of REALTORS®

… gives you the edge on the competition.

Dirk Zeller
President, Real Estate Champions

… a new standard for research on industry trends.

Bob Hale
CEO, Houston Association of REALTORS®

… where you go to find out what is GOING to happen.

Terry Watson
Speaker and Trainer

… a must read, every year.
Mark Willis
CEO, Keller Williams Realty International

SHIFTS SHAPING REAL ESTATE 2014-2018

SWANEPOEL

TRENDS
REPORT
2014

STEFAN SWANEPOEL

LIMIT OF LIABILITY / DISCLAIMER OF WARRANTY

While the publisher, authors, contributors and editors have used their best efforts in preparing this Report, they make no representation or warranties with respect to the accuracy or completeness of the contents of this report and specifically disclaim any implied warranties. The advice, strategies and comments contained herein may not be suitable for your market or situation.

Although the authors and contributors may, from time to time be an investor in companies mentioned in the Report, and most certainly serve as a consultants and/or advisor to numerous companies and organizations stated in the Report, the Report is written as a neutral, accurate and reasonable view of the industry and its participants. References to any companies, products, services and websites do not constitute or imply endorsement and neither is any reference or absence of reference intended to harm, place at a disadvantage or in any way affect any company or person. Information contained in this Report should not be a substitute for common sense, thorough research and competent advice.

As far as possible all statements, statistics and information included in this Report were verified with the parties mentioned or a credible source. Information is not treat and casually and great pride is taken to provide accurate information. The advice, strategies and comments contained herein may not be suitable for your market or situation and readers are urged to consult proper counsel or other experts regarding any points of law, finance, technology and business before proceeding. All conclusions expressed herein are also of course subject to local, state and federal laws and regulations. Neither the publishers, authors, contributors nor editors shall be liable for any loss or any other commercial damages, including but not limited to special, incidental, consequential, or other damages.

CONFIDENTIAL INFORMATION

No confidential sources were used in this Report and no information identified as confidential under any existing NDA was included without permission from the appropriate parties. This Report is a result of extensive research, articles that are readily available through the media, the study of hundreds of websites, Social Media pages, forums, surveys, whitepapers, and one-on-one discussions with industry decision makers, leaders, brokers, agents and vendors.

EDITOR IN CHIEF Stefan J.M. Swanepoel
COPY EDITOR Thomas Mitchell
CREATIVE EDITOR Tinus Swanepoel
TECHNICAL EDITOR DJ Swanepoel
WEBMASTER Alec Swanepoel
PUBLISHER RealSure, Inc.
EDITORIAL OFFICES
29122 Rancho Viejo Rd, Suite 201
San Juan Capistrano, CA 92675
949-481-9409
www.retrends.com

ISBN 978-0-9914076-0-6
PRICING $149.95 USA $159.95 CAN   €114.95 EUR

OTHER PUBLICATIONS
Swanepoel TRENDS Reports
- 2006, 07, 08, 09, 10, 11, 12, 13, 14

Swanepoel TECH Reports
- 2010, 2013

Swanepoel POWER 200

FIRST PUBLICATION ON TRENDS IN 1990

TRADEMARKS

Most of the companies mentioned in this Report own numerous trademarks and other marks and this Report, the publishers, the author, the contributors or any other party involved in this Report in any way seeks to challenge or dilute any of these marks. Specifically Realtor® is a registered trademark of the National Association of Realtors®.

IMAGES AND PHOTOS

All images not of specific people are protected by copyright and licensed by Shutterstock.

Table of Contents

Table of Contents

Table of Contents

144 CHAPTER 10 - CONSUMER FINANCIAL PROTECTION BUREAU

There are numerous federal and local entities and regulations that shape the residential real estate brokerage business and the home buying transaction, but this one could have the biggest impact we have seen in a long time. Throughout the history of organized real estate, and despite its key role in the U.S. economy, the marketplace has been largely free from federal regulatory interference (RESPA being a noticeable exception). The Consumer Financial Protection Bureau (CFPB), created in 2011 following the passage of the Dodd–Frank Wall Street Reform and Consumer Protection Act, however is potentially very different.

THE FUTURE OF THE BUSINESS OF REAL ESTATE —

AT THE ROCK FACE, ON WALL STREET, AND IN THE CLOUD

Over the years we have analyzed some 300 trends, published 4,000 pages of material, questioned over 5,000 agent/brokers, clocked more than 10,000 hours of research and written more 1,000,000 words. We know real estate trends like no one else, but still, nobody, including us, can predict the future.

The Future of the Business of Real Estate

In 2014 hundreds of new regulations created by the CFPB will become law, the majority of Prudential offices will convert to Berkshire Hathaway HomeServices, Redfin will most likely go public, Zillow or Trulia will pull off another astounding acquisition, Keller Williams Realty will pass 100,000 agent count, there will be a race by Realtors® to secure their dot REALTOR® high level domain, RE/MAX will buy back more of its regions, HomeServices of America will add another two great independents to their portfolio, and most agents will have a better year in sales than they did the last two years.

None of this is inside knowledge, merely extrapolations of activities and trends already visible and therefore fairly likely to occur.

In this chapter I give you my sense of where things are now and could be going in the future. It's interesting to make forecasts, even though it's hard as no one really "knows" the future. Some downplay trend tracking and some just throw out an opinion with unsupported conjecture. Then there are those of us that try our best to help recognize definable footprints that have been created. With meaningful research, analysis, thought, and yes, after two decades, thousands of companies and topics covered, and about a million words written in 25 books/reports we have shown that we can, with a high level probability, predict what is going to take place. Tracking trends is most certainly a complicated business, that's if you take it seriously like we do here at the *Swanepoel TRENDS Report* and Swanepoel T3 team.

We've constantly spoken about change and have cautioned about the transformation that is going to occur in the real estate business. Well, now more than ever before, the future doesn't feel that far away, it feels like the transformation is upon us.

GENERAL ECONOMY

The widely held view is that 2014 will be better than 2013, but barely. Interest rates remain low. Inflation is also still low. Oil continues to fluctuate but seems to be heading lower. Homeowners have equity in their homes again. Consumer confidence is much stronger. There is lots of pent-up consumer demand. The stock market is testing new record highs. Most companies are sitting on surplus cash. But companies are generally still gun shy after the previous recession and uncertainty still impacts most decisions. Acquisitions are therefore a safer bet than organic growth, so expect to see a large number of them, both outside (Google, AT&T, Cisco and Yahoo) and inside our industry (HomeServices of America, Zillow, Trulia, and RE/MAX).

THE BATTLE BETWEEN ONLINE AND OFF LINE

The Internet is generally considered to have entered the real estate brokerage business during 1994/5. That means we are now celebrating almost 20 years of incredible innovation. The pendulum has had time to swing from one extreme to the other and has with that sway pulled a

> 2014 will be faster and more fun than 2013.

stodgy "old" industry out of its hibernation into a fearless "new" world. And give credit where credit is due—the real estate business hasn't done all that badly. Many Thought Leaders have adapted to the digital (Internet, mobile, and cloud) race, and although they haven't all caught up, they have most certainly found a new middle ground between bricks and mortar and the cloud. Business has come to grips with the fact that there is value in having both physical stores and a strong Internet capability. The new normal is a competitive real estate marketplace where redesigned, reformatted, local, professional real estate offices co-exist alongside the Web to provide a fresh, fun, and fascinating home buying experience.

The mobility of connectivity has significantly changed the way in which the consumer searches for, finds, evaluates, and increasingly buys products and services. We have a legion of examples from books to movies, from airplane tickets to restaurants, and even cars and homes.

This evolution has caused the demise of some businesses like Circuit City, Borders, and Blockbuster, while at the same time causing the explosive growth of others like Google, eBay, and Amazon.com.

Real estate is undergoing a similar change and the *Swanepoel TRENDS Report* once again delves into and analyzes many of the essential and significant shifts.

CHANGING BUSINESS MODELS

The real estate business and business model is indeed a very unique one. In so many regards it's stodgy, slow responding, fiercely independent, and often times just outright stubborn. Yet it's also full of innovation, includes some of the country's most dynamic companies, and adopts various cutting edge technologies with vigor. And Realtors® have proven that when they decide to adopt a new service they do so rapidly and in droves.

THE CORPORATIZATION TREND MATERIALIZES IN SPADES

In the U.S. approximately 400,000 agents work for the 10 largest residential real estate franchise brands, of which some 250,000 agents are now affiliated with a public company (directly or indirectly through a publicly-traded holding company). That's a huge swing away from the more traditional "Mom and Pop" cottage type industry we had two decades ago. Most certainly over time this will gradually shift the industry to a more professionally managed corporate business environment.

The top three publicly held real estate groups/franchisors in our industry had a great 2013. After pulling off a tremendously successful IPO in 2012, Realogy Holdings Corp. (NYSE: RLGY) had a strong year-over-year increase in home sale transaction volume in 2013. No matter how you slice the numbers (office or agent count, sales volume or GCI) the collective numbers of all the brands under the

Realogy umbrella makes them the undisputed "Elephant in the Room." Their combined operations incorporate approximately 13,600 offices with 244,000 independent sales associates, which puts them #1 in the residential real estate business by a large margin.

HomeServices of America, a Berkshire Hathaway company (NYSE: BRK.A), completed its first year of operation after the acquisition of Prudential Real Estate Affiliates and Real Living late in 2012. In the short span of a few months late in 2013 they successfully converted tens of thousands of agents to the new "Burgundy and Cream" national brand—Berkshire Hathaway HomeServices. Although "conversions" will keep this group very busy for most, if not all of 2014, a high-end and commanding new brand in real estate has been born and will unquestionably be a major force for decades to come.

Netting some $225 million from a successful IPO in late 2013 (three times as much as Trulia's $89.4m or Zillow's $75.7m) this entrepreneurial driven business, RE/MAX (NYSE: RMAX), is still led by its co-founders (David and Gail Liniger) who continue to own approximately 61 percent of the company. RE/MAX is more frequently ranked number one in the real estate business than any other company and has been the highest ranked real estate company by Entrepreneur 10 times in last 14 years as well as ranked #1 the last four years in a row by Franchise Times. The Company is now more cash-rich than it has been in a long while and has indicated that it will accelerate its growth through acquisitions, especially by acquiring some regional real estate franchises in the Southwest and Mid-Atlantic regions.

ADDITIONAL FORCES TRANSFORMING THE BUSINESS

Various additional external forces—consumerism, connectivity, broadband, mobility, and capital—have steadily accelerated or matured in their own development cycle, each causing transformational and fundamental shifts in every industry. And, as real estate isn't exempt, the Internet, mobile phones, big data, and big capital are re-engineering our industry as well.

IPOs by portals Zillow and Trulia, and brokerage companies Realogy and RE/MAX, have led the acquisition of surplus capital. Redfin continues its impressive run of raising large amounts of capital, cloud-based eXP Realty reversed into a public company and new gen models like HomeSmart, Allison James, and @Properties are growing into substantial companies.

What will be interesting to monitor is whether or not this will have an impact on the perception of the best brands in real estate. As detailed in the previous edition of the *Swanepoel TRENDS Report*, branding is important, both inside and outside of the real estate business. According to Interbrand's annual Best Global Brand survey, long-time dominant brand Coke has slipped after being the number one brand for 13 years to the number three position, and Apple and Google have climbed to number one and two.

Although no similar survey is so widely recognized in the residential real estate business, three of the largest brokerage companies—RE/MAX, Coldwell Banker and

especially lift the mix of first-time buyers. Unfortunately, there is currently no certainty this will happen because the new guidelines for "qualified mortgages" will probably make lending harder, especially for minority and lower income earners.

ORGANIZED REAL ESTATE

I am more excited about the future of trade associations than I have ever been. Why? Because I believe there is for the first time widespread seriousness about the need and importance to do something of substance.

> The new normal is a competitive real estate marketplace where redesigned, reformatted, local, professional real estate offices co-exist alongside the Web to provide a fresh, fun, and fascinating home buying experience.

Century 21—are widely accepted as the best and most well known brands. However, they are being aggressively challenged by new real estate brands such as Zillow, Trulia, and Redfin (yes, I understand they are not brokerage brands but that is not the point), and a change in the industry's long standing dominance by franchise brands may occur in the not too distant future.

MORTGAGE MARKET

Wow, what a difference a year makes. We have come from being upside down only a few years ago (2007) to making profits between 2008 and 2013 that exceeded $200 billion. But maybe things are going to slow down for a while. In 2014, seven years after the subprime bubble, lenders will begin to operate under the new rules created through the 2010 Dodd-Frank overhaul and those created by the new Consumer Financial Protection Bureau (CFPB).

Various provisions of Dodd-Frank will become effective in January 2014 and hopefully they will be effective in helping lenders better understand what's required of them to properly underwrite a loan. Most banks would like to have more loans on their books, so let's hope this will

I believe Dale Stinton, CEO of the NAR, gets it better than any Association CEO before him, and above all he is willing to take the hard decisions. However, the difficulty is that it is not his sole decision to take. Many times I wish it was but, alas, time has sanctioned the evolution of a complex three-tier association structure.

The NAR has a board of directors of over 800 people making it one of the most unwieldy and uneconomical governing structures in the entire real estate world. Thought Leaders are most certainly talking taking about this dilemma but there is no method in place to resolve this very complex problem. A unanimous decision from the 800 to resign and step down, allowing a more effective board of 10 to be created, would be impressive, but very, very unlikely.

MEDIA

Overall newspaper adverting has fallen to an all time low, down 55 percent from its 2005 peak. On the other hand, Ad spending is growing again, particularly digital; online media and even TV. During 2013 we celebrated the 10th anniversary of MySpace and LinkedIn, two of the first leading Social Media networks, and yes, next year will be

Facebook's 10th anniversary as well. Social Media is now so ingrained that we just refer to it as Media.

The biggest Media buzz of the year went to high flying Twitter that pulled off a superb IPO with a 73 percent stock price pop on the first day that lifted the company's valuation past $20 billion—yes billion. To put that in perspective, that would be enough to buy (based on recent real estate IPO valuations) Coldwell Banker, Century 21, RE/MAX, Keller Williams, Prudential Real Estate Affiliates, Sotheby's, Better Homes and Gardens Real Estate, EXIT Realty, ERA Real Estate, and Weichert Realtors. Oh, and you could include Zillow, Trulia, Move, Inc., and probably the National Association of REALTORS® as well. That makes Twitter worth more than just about the entire residential real estate business. Go figure.

There is no question that (Social) Media has redefined the advertising landscape as consumers are increasingly sharing brand-related content and shopping experiences across an ever more open Web, including Facebook, Twitter, Instagram, and YouTube. So, better understanding of consumer-sharing behavior can help sellers, marketers, and sales people reach the right audience and engage them more effectively. The result would be

> There are always unknown places, but having a roadmap, even a partial roadmap, makes it easier than having none.

continued growth and a huge opportunity to see more marketing dollars, effort, and branding move further and deeper into online advertising.

Online networks, like Facebook, are aggressively exploring new digital approaches, platforms, and offerings to prove to companies in all categories that they have the reach and the methodology to identify and deliver any message directly to a targeted audience, probably better than any previous marketing or advertising vehicle.

THE YEAR 2013 IN NUMBERS

As these platforms gather more and more data on their users, their ability to target more directly is constantly being refined. Mistakes of today become the focus group stats of tomorrow. Look at some of the numbers that reached new landmark levels in 2013:

- There are over 150 million blogs of which WordPress hosts 75 million.
- LinkedIn passed 225 million, Twitter passed 500 million, and Facebook surpassed one billion users.
- Dropbox had more than 100 million users with one billion files uploaded daily.
- YouTube topped one billion monthly users.
- Instagram stored its four billionth photo while Flickr stored its eight billionth.
- YouTube enjoyed more than four billion daily views.
- Apple's customers downloaded over 50 billion apps.

INSIGHTS INTO BIG DATA ARE CRITICAL

Information and data, especially big data, is everywhere… but how do we make sense of what it is? How do we use all the data to really make a difference in sales, advertising, customer service, and so on? Selecting the right message, delivering it to the right consumer, at the right time and place still remains the holy grail of real estate marketing.

The new 24 x 7 x 365 anywhere environment has completely changed the rules regarding the marketing of homes and the attraction of potential homebuyers. According to NAR statistics, real estate professionals sell some five millions homes each year, and that means more than 400,000 buyers per month. Allowing for a generous scoop of looky-loos, you could easily double that number to one million people every month that are interested in homes.

By the end of 2013 Zillow announced that they had 60 million unique monthly visitors to their website browsing for homes; that's 6,000 percent more. Something's wrong or something's happened. Sure, one could debate the accuracy of any of the numbers, but that still doesn't account for an increase of 6,000 percent. What seems to be a very plausible argument is that the Internet and portals like Zillow, Trulia, and Realtor.com have exponentially grown awareness in real estate and almost single handedly created a huge new category of "home surfing." Awesome, but wait, the number of transactions didn't rise in any meaningful way, let alone with the same percentage. These people are really just looky-loos. It does; however seem that "home surfing" has become a "real" casual pastime... Interesting.

Consumers are finding a renewed enchantment with their home, the value, the trend line of their neighborhood/town/city, potential price qualities, features/services offered around their home, and so on. This is because a lot of this information about their home and neighborhood wasn't historically available to the average consumer. And yes, some people point to the fact that Realtors® kept the information private, and yes that is most certainly partially true. Significant chunks of the data were locked away in multiple silos (local authorities, title companies, etc.), but portions of it had simply just never been aggregated, mined, or scrubbed.

Now this new overabundance of services, apps, and information—some offered separately, some bundled with other services, and some delivered through existing brokerages companies—we are creating a fascinating new world of home-related data.

TOP CEOS WEIGHING IN

So this year, for the 2014 *Swanepoel TRENDS Report*, we decided to carefully select some of the smartest "Thought Leaders" in the real estate business to gain their views and opinions on the trends we're monitoring. We deliberately asked people who we knew had different vantage points and would therefore most likely put forth different viewpoints for the same questions. We also asked similar questions in slightly different ways. The respective responses were not shared between the contributors.

I am sure that most of you have by now come to appreciate the fact that I try to uncover all meaningful opinions and realistic scenarios without prejudging any

issue. So that's what we did this time in providing you with unfiltered opinions from all sides of the business spectrum. Savor the wisdom and experience from 60 of the industry's finest Thought Leaders—the majority of which are CEOs—who represent every corner of our industry, and collectively they indirectly represent our entire industry twice over.

In searching for whom we should invite to contribute we spent countless hours identifying the Thought Leaders, the Influencers, the Decision Makers, and the Power Players of our industry. As a result, we decided to share that research and information with you. No one has taken the time and effort to really try and create an objective, comprehensive list of, say the 200 most powerful people that shape our industry. So we thought, let's expand the value proposition of the *Swanepoel TRENDS Report* this year by providing the industry this service.

SWANEPOEL POWER 200 (SP200)

The Swanepoel Power 200 (SP200.com) now provides the most exhaustive list of Decision Makers, Thought Leaders, Influencers and Power Players ever assembled in the residential real estate brokerage business.

This list of 200 people include CEOs, other c-level

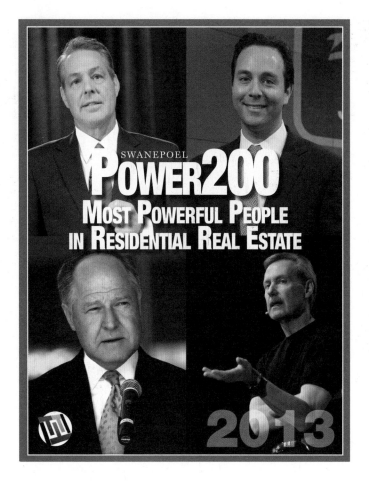

executives, broker/owners, authors, speakers, educators, economists, technologists, media executives, and even outsiders who impact the residential real estate brokerage business.

A team researched, investigated, cross-referenced, compared, studied, and spoke telephonically to, or personally connected with, many people on this list. We understand that there will always be more people to connect with and more people to add to the list—we intend to do that every year from now on—but this, the first SP200, will stand as a milestone and benchmark for the Power Players in our industry. These are the 200 people that individually and collectively make almost every significant decision that shapes our industry.

In the absence of comparable factual data we built our own database with information of each person, the position they hold within their company, the authority of the office they hold, their reporting line, their power and that of their company. And we looked at their national reach and clout, their industry-wide name recognition,

their personal influence and the substance, reach, and longevity of their contribution. Also, of importance, was the significance of their company, its overall geographical reach, financial strength, and the company's access to capital. For the first edition we have focused on just the United States and Canada.

Creating any ranking is challenging, but it's even more so when no corresponding, acknowledged public data is available. That's probably why our industry has never had an exhaustive list of the most powerful people ever published before. So we researched, analyzed, and reexamined this list from many, many different angles in an effort to produce a meaningful list. We understand that the SP200 isn't flawless and that everyone will have a different opinion. We would greatly appreciate your opinions and input to help us improve the SP200 and continue to build it into an asset the industry can use. So, please join us on Facebook at facebook.com/realestatetrends and share your thoughts.

To those Thought Leaders that have been included on the *Swanepoel Power 200*, we salute you and thank you for your contribution to our beloved industry. You are truly exceptional.

To those who did not find themselves on the list, whether you feel you should be on it or your time is yet to come, your contribution is also highly appreciated, and hopefully next year with the wind in your sails you may find yourself on this list of exceptional people.

A synopsis of the *Swanepoel Power 200* is included at the end of This Report, but for the full detailed SP200 list—all 40 pages—please go to SP200.com and download the complete *Swanepoel Power 200*.

The Swanepoel Group has for two decades tracked the trends, the changes, and the innovations in our industry. We've analyzed them, deliberated them, and published more books/reports on the topic of real estate trends than anyone else, so enjoy this, the 9th edition of the *Swanepoel Trends Report*.

Stefan Swanepoel

Analyst. Strategist. Trend Watcher. Industry Custodian.

***New York Times* Best Selling Author of 25+ Books and Reports**

CHANGES AND INNOVATIONS

Looking five to 10 years into the future is usually an exercise in futility. Looking three to five years is more realistic as that's how long it usually takes for trends to evolve from concept to mainstream. Furthermore as existing players are typically slow to change identifying the landscape over the coming years is fairly attainable. Well, at least we can try.

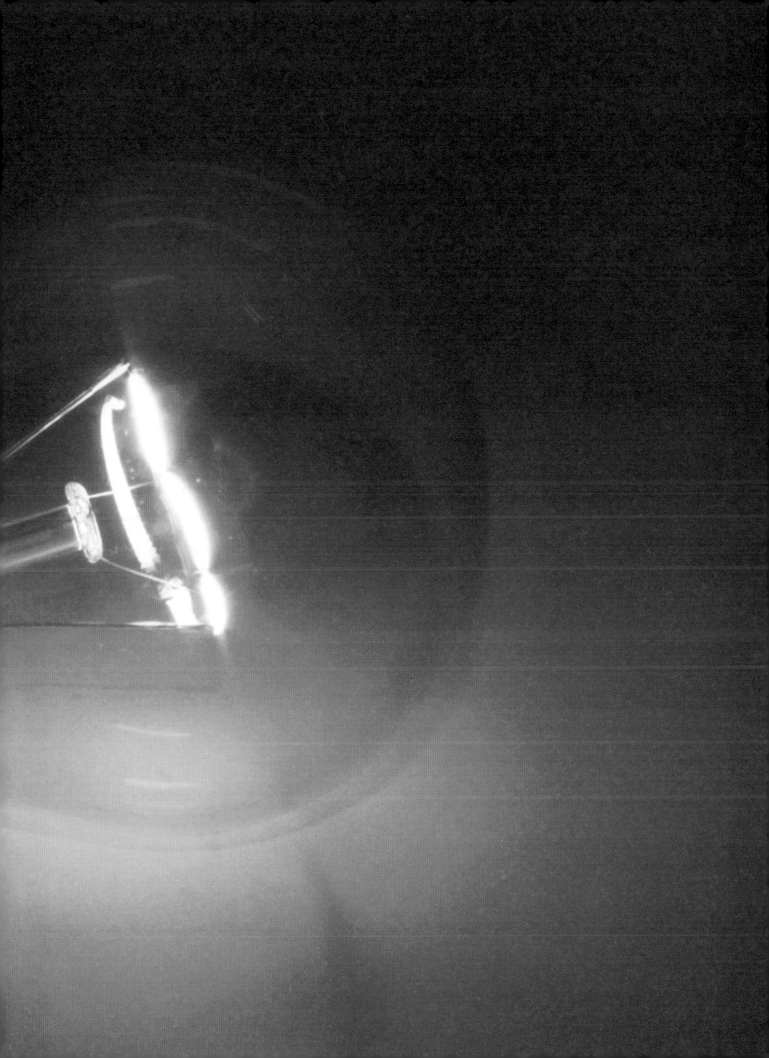

Changes And Innovations

Trends almost always follow an identifiable path. They usually also show that innovations frequently follow patterns. What I'm trying to say is that you can see the future if you look closely. The elusive part is the timing—the future always moves at its own pace—a part that is impossible to accurately predict. Sometimes it's dinosaur-like slow while at other times it explodes in an instant.

Good strategic thinkers can help to sketch out probable scenarios you should prepare for. You can do some of that yourself, with the help of the *Swanepoel TRENDS Report*. Take the best minds in your company and go lock yourself away somewhere—away from the daily distractions of phones and email. Read the last two or three *Swanepoel TRENDS Reports* and highlight what you think has a high probability of occurring. Consolidate the likeminded-identified items from within your group and see what bubbles to the top, Oh, and if you can afford it, do yourself a favor and get a good facilitator—it really does make a big difference.

So, for the first question in 2014 I selected a far-reaching and broad question. I wanted to start to sketch the overall canvass so the Thought Leaders included in this chapter were given the greatest free reign to respond to the broadest of all the questions.

Which three specific innovations/changes will, in your opinion, impact the residential real estate brokerage business the most over the next five years?

P.S. At the end of each of the chapter I will provide a summary and share my opinion. Enjoy.

QUESTION

Which three specific innovations/changes will, in your opinion, impact the residential real estate brokerage business the most over the next five years?

GARYKeller

Co-Founder and Chairman - Keller Williams Realty International

Since looking backwards is a great way to forecast forward, I see three events already underway that I believe will strongly impact the real estate industry in the next three to five years: agents expanding their borders, the expanded use of predictive analytics, and the progressing battle for online listing data.

Quite candidly, I believe the biggest innovation we will see in the next three years will not come from technologists, but from real estate agents themselves. Top agents who have crossed a certain production threshold are already monetizing their models, systems and administrative teams by expanding to new markets. These pioneers are struggling, but also finding success in doing exactly what real estate brokerages have been doing for decades—seeking additional profits by extending their reach. As the agent community begins to see what's happening and starts learning from each other this will go from the experience of a few into the opportunity of thousands, and in the process it will alter the look of our industry forever.

As part of this movement, some agents are also expanding their business by licensing their systems and products to other agents and brokerages. This is providing them with monetary compensation for their intellectual property and giving the licensee a leg-up with a fresh set of business tactics.

Another trend is towards personalization, which will undoubtedly have a huge impact on the way brokerages do business. In response to increasing amounts of information, agents are continuing to move their value proposition from "information provider" to "information interpreter." One way of making that transition is through a process of localization, where by becoming local experts agents are providing their customers with a trusting, personal experience.

Predictive analytics can add to the personal experience, just like it has in other industries. Similar to how Amazon generates 35 percent of its sales using suggested results, brokerages and individual agents will soon be able to provide buyers and sellers a higher level of relevant feedback that could make the home buying process more fluid.

The third trend on my list isn't new, but one that is ongoing—the battle over who will provide the public with their listing data. The biggest challenge with technology is that we tend to overestimate the short term effect and then when that doesn't pan out take a deep breath, step back and under-estimate the long term effect. Real estate agents and brokerages across the country are waking up to the reality that the current online listing marketing solutions aren't going to be the ultimate answer. Why? Because the Internet "by definition" wants to be a disruptor, and every day more and more attention is being drawn to the concept of disrupting the industry through how data for consumers is provided. This will not go away until the war is won. The outcome isn't decided at all, and brokerages are beginning to realize that if they don't step up and become the solution they will at some point become expendable. I believe the ultimate customer portal will come from within the industry.

BRADInman

Founder and Publisher - INMAN News

Here are three things going on right now that could change things in the years go come. How much, I do not know.

THE FLOOD OF CAPITAL
IS CHANGING REAL ESTATE

Real innovation comes when we have the ingredients that got us to the moon: money, brains and passion. In real estate today, these fundamentals are already in place.

A new generation of passionate leaders is taking over—younger and better educated agents, a new crop of innovative and fearless brokers, and a slew of start-up whiz kids. A recovering housing market and successful IPOs such as Zillow and Trulia are attracting super smart professionals who want in on the largess.

Indeed, capital has returned to the industry and that is a good thing. The largest real estate company, Realogy, has put a big dent in its debt and gone public with a fresh dose of capital ($1 billion with its IPO). RE/MAX has capital to invest as a result of raising $225 million with its successful IPO. One of the richest men in the world, Warren Buffet, is doubling down on real estate service with his Home Services franchise. Can Keller Williams be far behind, capitalizing its rapidly growing enterprise?

Then, there are the awe inspiring Zillow ($2.85 billion market cap) and Trulia ($1.25 billion market cap) IPOs. These two alone have a staggering amount of capital to invest in innovation, and stock prices that are perfectly poised for a slew of acquisitions. Then there is the ripple effect—dozens of new venture-backed companies.

So, how does this play out?

1. New and better products will be created. The sky is the limit on innovation.

2. Smaller tech companies will be gobbled up, as Realtor.com, Trulia, and Zillow square off in heated battle.

3. Brokers who don't innovate or partner will be left in the dust. Old ways are most threatened at times like this.

4. Agents will be offered more and more products and better ways to do their job. Their growing independence will be even more emboldened.

5. New business models will be tried, further challenging the old guard to innovate.

Finally and most importantly, the consumer will enjoy a better experience, buying, selling, and renting homes.

PARTNER OR DIE!

Every once in awhile, the currents are so right you can't ignore them. The real estate industry is at that moment today, those who get it will put fear aside and the risk will pay off. Change is happening so rapidly that no single company or individual can go it alone.

You need a channel partner for leads. You need a technology partner to deliver superior services. You need a team to close deals. You may need the right franchise partner to accelerate your brand. You need brokers and agents to sell products. And you need to make sure you build partnerships that create real, lasting value.

We are at a juncture that reminds me of the time when and why we started the INMAN Connect conference in 1997. Connect was about connecting the old world of real estate with the new world of tech innovation. Then, it was harder to make the connect case because the tech industry was naive and the legacy industry was full of fear. Today, we're at the same crossroads but for different reasons. The gains of partnering are overwhelming and a pre-requisite for success. Everyone is scrambling to do so and you must be part of the mix.

Trulia, Zillow, and Realtor.com need more and more agent and broker partners to grow revenue and to convince Wall Street that their sky-high valuations make sense. Franchises, brokers, and agents need Zillow, Trulia, and Realtor.com to deliver leads and sales. Small tech companies need brokers and agents who in turn need tech solutions to be more efficient, to offer more consumer products to their customers and more tools to close deals.

In my career, I was only as good as my partners. I thought that I had all of the answers, but success only came from bringing the right people together. INMAN News was built

> Change is happening so rapidly that no single company or individual can go it alone.

on the back of partnerships with Microsoft and newspaper giants. HomeGain succeeded on partnerships with the likes of Yahoo and Google. TurnHere depended on channel partners like AT&T and Yelp, and Vook depends on our relationships with publishers, literary agents, Amazon, and Apple.

Fear still abounds in the real estate industry, but those who let their worries consume them will fail—those who open themselves up, working with others will soar.

BROKERS ARE THE MOST THREATENED RUNG IN THE REAL ESTATE VALUE CHAIN

From the bottom, brokers are being squeezed by the growing independence of tech savvy real estate agents and brokers, and by portals that control the consumer relationship.

Innovation may not be the solution. Partnering may be their only option, unless their market share is so staggering that the threats are minimal. This will play out in a dramatic fashion over the next few years, as it has over the last ten. That is as much as I know for now.

CURTBeardsley

VP Product Marketing - Move, Inc.

The real estate industry will continue to be swept along in the steady flow of technology evolution, revolution, and innovation.

The following, in my mind, are potentially significant catalysts for disruption and change. In many cases, the impact is less from the innovations themselves, but from the opportunities these changes allow for in shifts in power—between large and small firms, agents and brokerages, traditional and new business models, etc.

For the last decade, many predictions have been made and many disappointments realized over anticipation of the consolidation of the fractured and inefficient MLS structures. In many ways, this infrastructure clutter has provided a much needed "barrier to entry" that allowed brokerages to maintain a foothold in the online world.

Today, several complete—or nearly complete—data compilations of nationwide listing data exist. Over the next few years, brokerages, software systems, and agent tools will begin to directly interact with these standardized compilations through APIs and direct interfaces—and not the underlying content providers (MLSs). This single access point for regional and national listing content will render the number or structure of these content providers largely irrelevant to the users. Many of these content provider systems will remain, but some brokerages will begin to directly interact with the aggregated compilations, relying on peer-to-peer and other alternative agreements for cooperation and compensation.

In addition to nationwide listing content, there will be a significant increase in the availability, depth of content and accuracy of property, property related information (neighborhood, schools, environmental, and demographic valuations and ratings), and the professionals involved in the transaction process. The key initial questions that potential home sellers and buyers currently ask of agents—how much is my home worth? or what more can you tell me about this home?—will largely be answered without personal interaction.

Home valuations (AVMs) will continue to improve

from work, my TV will automatically show me rich details of those properties when I walk into my home, while my tablet will pull up the profile of the companies and agents who are representing them.

The demand for high-quality media (photos, video, interactive floor plans) and the marketing and presentation skills to make a house as desirable online as it is off line are

> Single point access for regional and national listing content will render the number or structure of these content providers largely irrelevant.

with access to larger and more complete neighborhood and property profiles and will more completely take into consideration school and neighborhood desirability from consumer ratings and student scores: Home amenity improvements from local contractor and remodeler systems (the computer will actually have "seen" inside the home and know if there is granite countertops in the kitchen); and the intangibles like "curb appeal" and desirableness based on online consumer behaviors. This will drive the I need to contact an agent action even closer to the transaction—meaning the consumer will be more engaged and connected to the online brands they use during their pre-contact searching—and will give these online brands significant influence in who the consumer eventually engages with... if they do.

Lastly, there will continue to be a convergence in the personal technologies that are part of the integrated, multiscreen services that consumers will demand. The Smartphone will become the keystone, controlling and collaborating with the tablets, TVs and wearable technologies that are part of the consumer's digital lifestyle. We will no longer tolerate separate experiences using our 3, 13 or 60 inch devices, but expect a single experience that is uniquely tailored to the medium we're interacting with at any given moment. If I "like" a few homes that my phone highlights for me on my car's media screen on way home

going to segment and highlight the disparities in the service levels of the brokers and agents. How consumers can access and "consume" information will be as (or more) important as the source of the information (think Wikipedia vs. traditional encyclopedias), and the loyalty established with the providers of the experiences will be stronger than with the deliverer of the products and services (think Amazon vs. book publishers).

PAM O'Connor
President and CEO - Leading Real Estate Companies of the World

GLOBALIZATION

The world is shrinking, and as various economies ebb and flow, we have seen investment from foreign buyers increase to represent seven percent of all U.S. sales, and as much as thirty percent in states like Florida and California. Even in interior markets like Iowa's Quad Cities, multi-national companies are bringing in expats, so today's consumer wants to know that his or her home is exposed globally. Depending on how the U.S. economy grows or stagnates, residents here may also look to other countries to invest. Creating connections to other real estate professionals around the world, and developing platforms to achieve property exposure globally will become more prevalent as time goes on. This trend is already very much a factor in the luxury real estate market.

CROWDSOURCING — Consumer-generated content is a trend that is affecting how buyers get everything these days, from reservations at hotels and restaurants to plumbers. They trust the reviews of other consumers much more than traditional advertising, and they use them to validate their decisions as well, so brokerages that harness this trend will have a big advantage.

Crowdsourcing in real estate encompasses not only commentary about agent performance but also other website content like neighborhood insights (streetadvisor.com) and decorating tips (houzz.com). The more brokerages can engage consumers on their sites for this kind of content, the more they will be perceived as the "go to" source. And the more that brokerages focus on attracting and developing talented, competent agents who represent their brand extremely well, the more they will benefit from the reviews that are generated about those agents.

TRANSFERENCE OF WEALTH

Studies are showing that as Baby Boomers age, there will be a major transfer of inheritance to their children and grandchildren—much more than we have seen for generations. Those who inherit will be looking to buy homes—not necessarily large homes but multiple homes. This presents a tremendous opportunity to leverage the relationships with the Boomer generation to develop connections to their next-generation Millennials through referral introductions. While online resources, mobile technology and new-age forms of communication are critically important, the value of the off line referral to a trusted, competent advisor represents a huge opportunity to bridge the generations and capitalize on this transference of wealth trend that will gain traction over the next five to ten years.

The common denominator of all three of these trends is that ours is still a people-to-people business in which networks, relationships, and performance continue to be all-important, facilitated by online resources that foster a new era of transparency that will allow the best talent to surface and be recognized.

JACKMiller
CEO - T3 Experts

MILLENNIALS — Millennials Don't Care How You're Used to Doing Business. Millennials have grown up with technology that works remarkably well, and they won't suffer the industry's retro technologies—and retro mentalities—either as consumers or practitioners.

Millennials were born into an age of authenticity, bred and fueled by the rise of Social Media and a demographic-specific culture that reacts to polished marketing and advertising with indifference and sometimes even scorn. This generation won't be sold to the same old way, and it wants new interpretations of sales that are effective for them: reviews vs. sales presentations, being great vs. saying you're great, etc. Brokerages will either change to react to these realities, or new ones will emerge, that "make sense" to Millennials and their approach to technology, marketing, sales, and culture. Think "coffee shop meets Apple store," with a healthy measure of online sophistication.

MOBILE TAKES OVER

Agents and their customers will expect that all aspects of real estate are instantly available anywhere. If tools provided to agents and customers don't empower them to walk into a home, have access to all relevant data (comparable sales, public data records, etc.), and create an offer remotely with minimal technical expertise, you will be regarded a laggard in the market. Missing this will cost you customers as other agents and brokers beat you to the table with deals that don't wait for a trip back to the office. An entire ecosystem of mobile-enabled tools is rapidly maturing, and soon will become the primary tool set of the industry. In two to three years, a new crop of vendors will replace the "old world," and the mobile experience will be as important as the desktop for both agents and customers.

BIG DATA MAKES THE IMPOSSIBLE POSSIBLE

In the next two to three years, the tools agents use will leverage consumer credit data, Social Media activity, email open/click data, web browsing action—even phone call data—to produce robust views of an agent's customer database, and to create competitive capacities for prospecting and target marketing. Tools that do some of this already exist, and we're about to see a lot more. Applications utilized by customers—next gen website and search tools—will be aware of friend networks, lifestyle preferences and location to make the user experience rich. Features like following and commenting on your friends' home searches, or being alerted of nearby amenities that match Social Media profile preferences will be taken for granted.

Real estate tools built with integration-oriented platforms will dominate the space, taking advantage of big data and providing these new features. These tools will provide a software capabilities landscape previously thought impossible (sorry if that sounds ambiguous, but it's impossible to predict exactly how this is going to play out). In the near future, software and data will merge into a sophisticated symphony that we're just now beginning to imagine. Perhaps somewhat ironically, the end result of this trend will likely be a shift in terms of the focus of the agents' role away from technical tactics and back in the direction of softer skills like relationship building and selling.

GAHLORDDewald

Founder - Thoughtfaucet

When I think of innovation what I'm really looking for is how human behavior changes. It isn't truly about the technology, or the widget, or the gadget, or any of the other stuff we read about in the popular press. Innovation is really about change in human behavior—not the latest shiny object.

So when I think about innovations for the residential real estate practice in the five years ahead what I focus on is what changes will happen in three core groups of people: consumers (people buying and selling residential real estate), real estate professionals (agents, brokers, and their dedicated support teams), and "all those other services involved in the transaction" (banking, title, etc). For something to be innovative it will need to result in changes in behavior in one or more of these three groups.

There is some of what I call "topographical" change happening in these groups, things that set the landscape in which any potential innovation will operate. For example, as Millennials continue to age into the workforce for the real estate professional segment and the consumer segment they bring with them some realities. Their student

debt, their second-row seat to the most recent boom/bust cycle of real estate, and their having lived the majority of their lives in a digitally connected world are just three that will have strong influence on anything that happens in real estate for those who work with that demographic (or with properties that appeal to that demographic).

Hold that thought for a moment while I switch gears to another topographical item: socially enabled technology. For the past 15 years digital technology has been developed for a mass audience.

On the front end, socially enabled technology has

been a successful innovation. Email, digitally-enhanced text, chat, social networks, etc have all become quite embedded in the way many people communicate today. On the back end, socially enabled technology has been doing what digital technology does best: gather data. What began as server stats and transformed into web analytics is now in the process of growing into deeper layers of knowledge and insight generation about the people who use socially enabled technology.

The social networks and communication tools we use today are simply inputs absorbing our real world lives into something quantifiable in the digital realm. Our photos, our correspondence, our preferences, our locations, our friends are all being pushed into the socially enabled

> Socially-enabled technology has been a successful innovation.

technology systems. Our behaviors are being digitized. This includes real estate behaviors.

So let's consider these two topographical aspects at play in the next five years. On one hand we have a generation that has lived an entirely digitized life, staring down 30 or even into their mid-thirties. On the other hand we have a technology that has been present in their lives recording any and all data points that have been volunteered.

An innovation that I see coming along will exploit this topography is the methods of statistics, predictive analytics, and especially network analysis that will be brought to bear in order to influence this and future generations in a myriad of ways. This will go well beyond today's ad retargeting or recommendation engines. For example, the data that is being volunteered and gathered today will be useful in predicting productivity in the workforce. Most of the people I meet in the real estate industry note how important sphere of influence is in the

success of their business. A broker may change the way he or she works with an agent based on an analysis of an agent's social network. If one were to callously consider their social network a gold mine, social network analysis might reveal how rich a vein it is. Knowing this, an agent may change the nature of how they develop social relationships in order to become more profitable.

On the consumer end, the volume of data gathered about their preferences well before they even know they are looking to buy or sell property will be used to facilitate a transaction. The application of predictive analytics on behaviors correlated to real estate will be leveraged. The mechanism for this innovation is the shift of socially enabled technology from being a data repository that is only lightly utilized today into data-driven decision support systems.

The fly in the ointment is, of course, that not everyone in the industry will have access to these resources. While it will require money as one aspect of resource the other, which is perhaps even more important, is the actual data itself. Few players in the industry today have access to the amount and type of data required to make the shift into decision support systems. Even fewer of those players are residential real estate brokers or agents. This will create cracks in the topography that allow for significant disruptions among competing brokerages/agents and perhaps business models as well.

SUMMARY, Opinion and TakeAway

Looking at the views from the "Thought Leaders," one cannot help but be struck by the overwhelming sense of the "Possible." Even the most cynical observer feels hope for the future. As a firm believer that there is always an option not yet considered and always a solution to every problem/challenge, I love that.

The overall picture painted is a world in which the new, ever-connected, real estate advisors (one can hardly call these new real estate professionals mere agents or sales associates or Realtors® anymore) uses the cloud, mobile-everywhere, data-mining, predictive analytics, and detailed information on each and every property. They are using near-virtual reality and automation to create a consumer experience that will be as easy and simple in the near future as it is difficult and painful today.

It appears that most of the predictions about innovation center around—or at least firmly have in mind—the Millennials, the Most Important and Most Connected Generation Ever! Most of the visions at least invoke the consumer habits of the Millennial who is more comfortable texting her best friend, even if she's sitting across the lunch table.

It does appear that the zeitgeist around innovation today involves some mixture of mobile, big data, and predictive analytics. Those three major technology shifts interact with the rise of Millennials to suggest that brokers and agents must adapt to the new consumer mindset and behavior. For example Jack Miller, former CTO of the GoodLife Team, stated that:

Millennials have grown up with technology that works remarkably well and they won't suffer the industry's retro technologies—and retro mentalities—either as consumers or practitioners.

Real estate is one of the most conservative, established, and above all, regulated industries in the U.S. In other Trend Chapters (4 and 10), we see evidence that while leaders dream of revolution, the fundamentals of our beloved industry are very stable and well entrenched, as a resulting only moving with incremental change.

Big data and predictive analytics in housing are possible today, except that a bewildering array of copyright claims (currently being contested in courts), industry rules, and federal, state, and local laws and regulations make accessing the data problematic. Of course the entire topic of listing data—who owns it, who can do what with it and where and how—is something of a hot topic within the industry. The Big Data revolution in real estate is hardly possible without access to data, and that is no certain thing in today's environment.

We hope that Curt Beardsley, SVP of Realtor.com, is right when he says that we will have solved the data access problem within the next five years, but so far the industry track record seems to indicate that we probably will not. Therefore we believe that until all the major data issues are resolved, most of the technology innovations that so many of us hope for will remain visions rather than reality.

The one possible exception that will most likely occur sooner and with more certainty is predictive marketing analytics, drawn from mining social data. As Gahlord Dewald said:

A broker may change the way he or she works with an agent based on an analysis of an agent's social network. If one were to callously consider their social network a gold mine, social network analysis might reveal how rich a vein it is. Knowing this, an agent may change the nature of how they develop social relationships in order to become more profitable.

Some form of social data mining and predictive analytics will see the light of day in the next few years. Unlike real estate listing data, a person's social graph and behavioral data are all available from a variety of vendors and sources, often in real-time. There are no industry wars there, so the data is available, if at a cost.

It seems likely that one or more of the major technology companies with the financial and technology resources to mine that personal social and behavioral data for real estate will develop usable tools that allow for much more personalized and efficient marketing of brokerage services, if not of property. However, service delivery and

who is also the founder of one of the largest and most successful real estate companies, believes this is a trend developing, we're inclined to follow his lead.

Also we like Brad Inman's wisdom that success in the future will depend on partnering with the right people. As the scope of the market expands, the industry will become more specialized and better funded, and as the players become larger this move will prove itself to be today's reality.

And we can't leave this section without mentioning one of our favorite predictions, and one that is most likely to come about. Pam O'Connor, CEO of Leading Real Estate Companies of the World, believes that intergeneration wealth transference will provide the next big wave of opportunity. We agree that this change will profoundly impact the industry. The tough call, however, is whether it will be over the next five years since the oldest Baby Boomers are just hitting 67 and most of them are still a ways away from retirement. Leaving inheritances behind may not yet be on their table.

property marketing will likely require that the real estate listing data issue be resolved.

There is also a real feasible innovation in the near-term that may come from business model changes, rather than from new technology. Gary Keller, one of the best strategic thinkers the industry has ever had, is on to something when he says that top agents are extending their reach and business models:

These pioneers are struggling, but also finding success in doing exactly what real estate brokerages have been doing for decades—seeking additional profits by extending their reach. As the agent community begins to see what's happening and starts learning from each other this will go from the experience of a few into the opportunity of thousands, and in the process it will alter the look of our industry forever.

If the author of *The Millionaire Real Estate Agent,*

As stated before, predicting and analyzing the trends, scoping out different possible scenarios, and then preparing business and action plans to prepare for the change, is not only wise, but can be done with a fairly high level of probability. Remember the hardest part, by far, is to correctly predict the timeline the future will evolve, arrive, be accepted by mainstream, and/or gain broad mass appeal.

BROKERAGE BUSINESS MODELS

In acknowledging the muscle of technology, the Internet, mobile and the cloud one must also accept that the same power will change the existing paradigm and business model.

Brokerage Business Models

The past three editions of the *Swanepoel TRENDS Report* have separately and thoughtfully examined the real estate brokerage business model, from franchising structures to entrepreneurial innovation, and from office configurations to recipes for success.

We have, as is our guiding principle, tried to be inclusive of options rather than exclusive. We have stretched your mind to consider the unusual and different while acknowledging the existing value proposition of the prevailing models. Change is never always good or bad, but it's real.

So in acknowledging the muscle of technology, the Internet, mobile and the cloud we must accept that it will change the existing paradigm. For example more companies in the real estate vertical have, in the last two decades, become owned by a public entity or have followed the IPO route than in any other period in history. In addition, a large number of new players (portals) have entered the industry and have quickly created billion dollar enterprises.

The concern is, whether existing companies will restructure and readjust sufficiently to remain the industry's largest and most powerful players. Or will they move too slow and allow the new players to grab a disproportionate market share and/or redefine the rules and/or reslice the pie? If history is anything we should learn from, then the latter is the more probable.

So the question poised was deliberately very general along wide interpretation so that when you read it, it kindles your own thinking. Here is what we said to Thought Leaders:

QUESTION

Over the next three to five years, which broad category of brokerage business model (not a specific company or brand) is expected, in your opinion, to show the most significant growth? Use any parameter(s) you wish; agent count, office count, sales volume, profitability, etc.

a) Local Independent brokerages.

b) Global franchise brands/networks.

c) Virtual and Cloud-based companies.

d) Any other model you would like to identify (describe model)

ALEXPerriello

President and CEO - Realogy Franchise Group

During the next three to five years, I anticipate that global franchise brands/networks are the business model that will show the most significant growth. The residential real estate industry is currently in the midst of a wave of brokerage consolidations, with a high percentage of broker/owners at (or past) retirement age who are now trying to time their exit from the business.

Look at it this way, if you are a long-time brokerage owner just now considering retirement, you've survived the housing downturn so you're most likely looking for two things in the process. First, you want a way to monetize the value of your business and all the sweat equity you put in through the years. Second, you also want to do right by and for the people who helped you build your business, so finding the best possible environment for your sales associates to thrive in an increasingly high-tech marketing environment is a key consideration.

Franchised firms are typically larger companies, with a heavy focus on marketing, technology, and training. Given that these types of larger companies are the ones who are actively looking to expand their presence via mergers or acquisitions during the upswing of the housing market recovery, all indicators point to further growth in real estate franchise affiliations during the coming years.

At the same time, new brokers entering the business are extremely tech-savvy and brand-conscious, which gives them an appreciation for franchising. They understand that consumers respond favorably to powerful brands. When top agents make the move to become broker/owners, these new brokers are looking to established franchise brands to help jump start their progress as they build their business. According to the *2013 NAR Profile of*

Real Estate Firms, 87 percent of firms reported their current franchise affiliation improved their firm name recognition, 85 percent reported an improved use of technology, and 83 percent reported an improvement in acquiring listings.

The same NAR survey also indicated that 85 percent of real estate firms are independent companies, while the latest annual NAR Member Profile reports that 60 percent of all Realtors® (agents) are unaffiliated with any franchise. Thus, either way you look at the opportunity, there remains considerable long-term upside growth potential for global franchise brands in the real estate industry.

DANDuffy
CEO - United Real Estate

The "right conditions" for innovation of real estate brokerage models has existed for at least fifteen years; so, why hasn't there been any truly innovative, disruptive business models emerge as a market share leader to challenge the status quo?

It's simple. The established models and those that are benefiting most from deferring innovation (franchisors and SOME brokers) resist change and defend their economics at the expense of those that would most benefit from these changes (clients and agents).

We all resist continual, disruptive innovation at our own peril. History is littered with business models in every market segment that waited too long to change (e.g., Blockbuster, American Airlines, Kodak). External conditions for innovation left unaddressed allowed curious, innovative companies to enter incumbent's markets and cause significant business disruption at best and many times outright collapse.

Darwin would have a lot to say about this phenomenon. He would observe that real estate brokerage models have been in an extended period of stasis, where things don't change much for an extended period of time. He would also observe that the real estate industry is currently experiencing a moment primed for punctuated evolution—a sudden change where conditions allow for major improvement in fitness—due to environmental conditions in our market. Not the least of these environmental conditions are dramatic changes in client behavior and market power shifts—from franchisors-to-affiliated brokers, from brokers-to-agents and from agents-to-clients—brought on by advances in technology and a democratization of information flows.

So given all of this, what does the brokerage model of the future look like? What attributes must be present to be competitive and profitable over the next decade?

Enable agents to make a great living—100 percent compensation plans and extremely low fees are a must without forcing the agent to compromise on broker support. To accomplish will require a really efficiently run business and passing the lion's share of the efficiency gains along to agents, This is an area where the real estate franchisors must and will step up to remain relevant.

Be highly differentiated in areas that are important

to clients, communicate these differences to the market and avoid competing on commoditized and easily matched "antes" or worst yet size—If all of your competitors offer the same services who cares? They're just your ante to enter the game. Remember, clients don't care if you're bigger than the next brokerage firm or "global network" with superior, tangible marketing techniques and tools or specialty niche or market expertise.

demand this as they discover their market power.

- Affiliated Network or Franchise—scale is required to deliver the shared services at the price points required.

- Lead Aggregator—technology allows scaled networks to do this in house vs. relying on third parties

While we have danced around this for over a decade, the conditions for creating a "blended" model

> We all resist continual, disruptive innovation at our own peril.

Be hyper efficient controlling overhead cost structure.Brokers must remove the burden of excessive lease expenses for unneeded or unwanted space, franchisor royalties and fees that are excessive vs. the value derived from their services, and they must leverage technology to reduce administrative support expenses without compromising support offering.

Reduce the procurement costs of all required resources to operate the brokerage. There will be a substantial consolidation of those vendors providing technology and other services to brokerages and costs will come down drastically: i.e., lower unit cost per agent of a comprehensive technology platform, insurance, training, transaction management, etc.

Maintain absolute alignment in outcomes between the success of agents and that of the brokerage.

Manage the brokerage manner consistent with a clear vision, well defined and articulated guiding principles and have an intense curiosity and commitment to constant improvement.

Using the terms in our industry today, the brokerage described above is a hybrid of the following four brokerage / business models:

- 100 percent commission / low fees—to address need to improve agent economics and alignment.

- Full Service Plus—clients and agents are and will

that incorporates the best aspects of each of the leading brokerage business models are present today. Someone will assemble these pieces and dramatically change the real estate marketplace for the better for all stakeholders.

GINOBlefari

President and CEO - Intero Real Estate

A new model will need to have a global brand that represents success as well as integrity and is recognized nationally as well as internationally. The off-the-top fee paid by the agent would not only fund the brand but would also build in a guaranteed return on revenue for the company.

WEALTH BUILDING/AGENT COMPENSATION - The core business model would be set up to help agents run their business more efficiently, effectively, and profitably. The new model will need to have a wealth building component that creates collaboration companywide.

But this collaboration can't simply be agent-specific or branch-specific; it must be companywide to include a sales executive's ability to financially benefit from all the vertical and horizontal growth of their company.

The underlying wealth building philosophy would be: "What's good for the company is ultimately good for the agent and what's good for the agent is ultimately good for the company." Compensation plans will need to be market sensitive as well as business flexible, which means the need to provide different compensation programs for different size agents.

TECHNOLOGY - Overall, technology is made up of ever-changing tools. These tools need to continue to be relevant over the short and long term. A firm will need to have the ability to switch to the most relevant technology at the time it makes sense to do so, as opposed to building a model on a particular technology type, which would make it very difficult to stay relevant over the long haul. The ability to generate leads that are passed down to the agent will be an important piece of the technology tool.

TRAINING - The new model will need to provide sales executives with a much higher level of instruction and business acumen. You will need to have a deep understanding of a specific agent's needs, their strengths, weaknesses, and the outcomes they want to achieve. Your training and coaching will need to be specific, measurable, and have an accountability measure to it.

PEOPLE - The new model will need to take into account that the personal life and business life of an individual agent are unavoidably intertwined. It will create a business/life consultant role for company leadership. Some of the support will be internal with other support being outsourced yet need to be managed internally.

PHILANTHROPIC - The new model will need to be sensitive to the community and be philanthropic. The underlying philanthropic philosophy would be: "As realtors we earn our living by serving our community so it is fundamental in the creation of this new model that we find a way to give back to the community."

MICHAEL McClure

COO - T3 Experts

In terms of real estate brokerage models, the future ultimately belongs to the "true virtual" concepts—the companies with absolutely no brick and mortar. This model will grow the most in coming years because...

- Technology has already advanced to the point where agents don't need to work in offices. Tablets and Smartphones have reached a level of sophistication that allows every aspect of a transaction—from running CMAs and comparables to writing offers to obtaining digital signatures to handling the entire contract-to-close process—to be done anywhere.

- A generation of digital natives is coming of age and will soon become the dominant real estate demographic (both in terms of clients and agents). This demographic places little credence on "the status quo," and many are remote workers and entrepreneurs themselves don't see value in or the need for a traditional office setting.

- Margins in real estate are thin. The operating expense differential between a virtual office and a traditional brick-and-mortar office is typically significant. Once

brokers realize that the next generation of agents won't care much if at all about having an office, there will be a wholesale shift to virtual simply because it is financially advantageous.

- F2F (face-to-face) technologies like Skype and Google Plus Hangouts make it easy for people to work together virtually. These advanced communication tools are excellent surrogates for the handful of F2F meetings that agents have with brokers in a given month or quarter, and for the handful of in-office F2F interactions an agent usually has with their client during the arc of a typical transaction (mainly preliminary consultation and executing offers).

- Doing business at a Starbucks is now a completely accepted part of our culture. Ergo, free alternative offices exist on every corner, and with online banking the movement of money—to disburse a commission or deposit an earnest money check—is as easy as downloading and using an iPhone app anywhere, anytime.

- Real estate is inherently transient and most agents— even those who call themselves "traditional"— typically spend the majority of their time away from their offices. It's just the nature of the job.

It may take longer than three to five years for this model to reach its maximum growth potential for two main reasons: 1) an aging/older agent demographic that will likely slow the adoption rate of full virtual, and 2) the many brokers caught in long-term leases and or franchise agreements that require a physical office configuration of some variety. But the real question is not IF ... but WHEN...

GLENNSanford

Founder and CEO - eXP Realty

"Honey, I'm heading into the office" may take on new meaning in the next five years. As we agents, brokers, sales managers, and owners continue to adopt more and more collaborative technologies the question is, where does the office actually exist? It seems to me in three to five years the office will essentially be paperless, and the bricks and mortar of the traditional office will be as redundant as the phone app is on our current Smartphones. Yes, a physical office will still provide value, but to those who investigate online collaborative infrastructures there are so many other ways to work together

that the physical office will likely be a luxury rather than a necessity. It will just be there because of some ongoing perception that the clients or agents want an office to go to. The reality is that the traditional real estate office has grown tired and those who aren't adapting will continue to have challenges attracting agents and consumers alike.

Forward thinking companies have been moving more and more of their core business functions into the cloud. It doesn't hurt that there are plenty of cloud-based offerings for brokerages to choose from, some of which are just shiny objects and some that truly change what it means to collaborate. Google Chat and

Hangouts represent a light version of quick conversations whereas richer more immersive technologies like WebGL technologies (like those offered by CloudParty) will likely take center stage with the ability to "see in" to the office from anywhere on any device. Knowing that someone is free to meet will likely be acknowledged by some sort of Avatar showing that they are available and not presently involved in any other conversations. At some level this Avatarness will also translate into the consumer/agent interaction. Gartner Research popularized the Emerging Technology Hype Cycle showing where a technology triggers create a period of Inflated Expectations, followed by

both the totally cloud-based models that have the potential of totally disrupting what it means to be a real estate brokerage. When a brokerage can operate without bricks and mortar and still provide all the infrastructure that one would expect that does represent the holy grail of what the Internet first promised 20 years ago with the launch of NCSA Mosaic and the World Wide Web. The promise of lowering costs to the brokerage while providing better and faster information to agents and consumers is the promise that is already being delivered by a number of companies and technologies. I think we all know it's coming, however only a small few will be able to take advantage of it and

> Consumers will soon be able to see the availability of an agent from any device, whether surfing through the various MLS listings on the brokerage website or some other listing aggregator website.

the Trough of Disillusionment and then an upward Slope of Enlightenment through the Plateau of Productivity. In 2012 Virtual Worlds for business was on the Slope of Enlightenment Stage and the prediction by Gartner is that it will reach the Plateau of Productivity stage in the next five to ten years.

Consumers will soon be able to see the availability of an agent from any device, whether surfing through the various MLS listings on the brokerage website or some other listing aggregator website. It wouldn't surprise me if a new listing aggregator emerges that embraces enhanced imaging technology along with WebGL to augment property listings in ways we haven't yet imagined. There is at least one company that is developing a camera that brings Google Street style views to home walkthroughs. Imagine consumers walking through homes on their computer rather than looking at static 2D photos.

Of course the question is and will be where is the office? Is it physical bricks and mortar, is it the virtual office or is it a combination of both. Though without a doubt, the latter state of most offices today is some combination of

really capitalize on it. Even now, 20 years later, it's still the wild frontier with regard to technology and I for one am excited because of the journey and the opportunity.

MICHAEL Kidd

EVP - Orlando Regional REALTOR® Association

Economic geography in an era of global competition is a growing paradox for the governance and the business of the organized real estate services industry. It is widely recognized that changes in technology and competition are diminishing many of the traditional roles of location.

Inasmuch, the organized real estate services industry— the trade associations and the transaction marketing mediums (multiple listing services)—will have to emulate the markets their members exist in or they will cease to hold a relevant attraction to those in the market. Specifically, the Realtor® business models maintained in the association and multiple listing arenas will need to shift away from the NAR's long-standing governing structures with its synthetic boundaries (chartered locations) of "local/state/national," which restricts business growth and potency, to a more organic relational range focused on the economic realities, markets, and relationships that are now very much "regional/national/global" in nature.

Look at the boom in international real estate programs, conferences, and membership groups. These business interests have no intent on refraining from a transaction because it may cross a county line, a state line, or a country border. Associations and related membership support services will have to take into account the number of real estate professionals who are partnered with others in distant regions and countries. These long-distance business relationships do not stop at local county lines or city limits, and they will not stand still with service organizations that wear such handcuffs.

Further complicating the real estate service industry is the fact that Realtor® Association Boards and independent MLS companies are very much in competition for the very same precious assets; members' time and the commodities that comprise the "membership market." Unfortunately, most won't admit that there is real competition for these assets and thus go about the political side of the business, which is an inevitable ingredient in the membership market, and in passive aggressive fashion, undermine one another. Quite frankly, a shift in governance and market range may not be possible until we

that capitalize on Realtor® market activities and needs. They are able to offer more product and service due to a regional (membership) posture and size—primarily what association boards are supposed to accomplish by wielding the power and size of their memberships.

The irony is that Realtor® Directors of MLS company boards are aggressively seeking and successfully capturing larger markets, often at the expense of local association boards while the same Realtor® Directors of Association Boards hold tightly to dated practices, egotistical fiefdoms, and diminishing business relevancies.

> Until a more organic service range is acknowledged, examined, and reasonably re-tooled, the losses and gains in the organized real estate service industry will be at the expense of Realtors® and the business models they created.

openly admit and accept that we are indeed in competition.

There is a need to reposition the real estate service and product industry in the spirit of "co-opetition" and create a value net (think of the relational value of hardware and software) that focuses on membership market efficiencies and relations. Our current location driven strategies focus on local market domination which is currently causing market fragmentation and, subsequently, costly inefficiencies and a huge amount of frustration for the brokers who shoulder the costs.

The paradox in our present situation is that the very same people driving MLS strategies—Realtors® elected or appointed to director positions on MLS boards— are often the very same elected and appointed association board directors that are hand-cuffing association business strategy. For example, many MLS companies are expanding, pursuing regional markets and economies of scale, which is necessary to survive and thrive in today's "membership market." These companies are benefiting from larger markets, using their numbers to expand into the consumer's conscience and therefore, into new markets

If the association board business model is going to survive in the membership marketplace, it too must follow the trends, benefits, and efficiencies of regionalization. Some might call this "merging or consolidation," which fuels a fear of loss for many Realtor® Directors on Association Boards while expansion and mergers are sought with the expectation of "gain" by those on MLS boards.

Until a more organic service range is acknowledged, examined, and reasonably re-tooled, the losses and gains in the organized real estate service industry will be at the expense of Realtors® and the business models they created.

CAMERONMerage

President and CEO - First Team Real Estate

At the same time consumer expectation in terms of their agents'/brokers' value proposition is rising in conjunction with continuing downward pressure on commission rates, especially where there is inadequate perceived value received.

This in turn has caused agents to question their brokerage company's value proposition and place upward pressure on commission splits paid to agents who provide inadequate value. This has eroded brokerage profitability with fewer resources available to support and improve the agents' ability to compete by driving added value to their customer base vs. lowering their fee to compete.

> More than ever before there is an intensified and evolving gap between price and value in all aspects of our industry.

More than ever there is an intensified evolving gap between price and value in all aspects of our industry. Whereas in the past long term relationships between agents and clients on the one hand, and brokerages and their agents on the other, was substantially based on strength of personality, more and more today there is a demand for the delivery of quantifiable value. To compete in the current innovative economy, just coming up with innovations isn't enough.

I see more significant changes taking place than innovations. Today there are plenty of innovations already in the industry but the brokerages and agents aren't adequately applying these to add value to their customer base and better position the companies and agents to meet or surpass customer needs.

In fact, there are already plenty of innovative tools available; however it's sorting out the application of the most appropriate innovations in technology, marketing, training, and other areas that counts. What will matter is the leveraging of innovation to create added value in order to stay on the edge of consumer and agents' demand.

SUMMARY, Opinion and TakeAway

As one would expect, those who lead companies have total confidence in their respective business models. Large independent brokers believe that they will emerge victorious, while global franchise executives stress the utter importance of having international reach in today's connected world. And the companies who bet on virtual offices and cloud-based workflow believe that both of those other guys are dinosaurs unprepared for the coming Ice Age.

They are also, of course, all correct.

Change is very seldom a sheer cliff that one day a company unexpectedly crosses and falls to their immediate doom and disappears. Yes, I know that some may like to point to the disasters of a Borders and how Amazon crushed them, and how Netflix destroyed Blockbuster, when allegedly, everyone but they saw it coming. But, upon in-depth research and analysis you understand that there were additional reasons why things occurred. There were different shifts in play and multiple circumstances that led to certain events occurring. And we also look past the many companies that were in a similar position but did change and weren't destroyed in the same way.

One of the most powerful people in the entire residential real estate industry, Alex Perriello, CEO of Realogy Franchise Group, points out some rather pertinent facts about growth opportunities for global franchises, citing the *2013 NAR Profile of Real Estate Firms:*

- 87 percent of firms reported franchise affiliation improved their firm name recognition
- 85 percent reported an improved use of technology
- 83 percent reported an improvement in acquiring listings.

Since 65 percent of brokerages are independents and 60 percent of Realtors® are unaffiliated with any global brand, Alex sees huge opportunity ahead, especially as the economy improves.

Of course, one would expect Dan Duffy, the CEO of new business model franchise United Real Estate, who believes the old guard is vulnerable to disruption would take a different view, and he does:

Darwin would have a lot to say about this phenomenon. He would observe that real estate brokerage models have been in an extended period of stasis, where things don't change much for an extended period of time. He would also observe that the real estate industry is currently experiencing a moment primed for punctuated evolution—a sudden change where conditions allow for major improvement in fitness—due to environmental conditions in our market. Not the least of these environmental conditions are dramatic changes in client behavior and market power shifts—from franchisors-to-affiliated brokers, from brokers-to-agents, and from agents-to-clients—brought on by advances in technology and a democratization of information flows.

And from the ranks of the cloud-based companies, Glenn Sanford, the CEO of eXp Realty, would find himself within these kinds of thoughts. He points out, and of course we all agree, that technology hasn't just fundamentally changed consumer behavior, it's changed the way we all work. Consumers want information and service immediately over the latest wireless and web communication channels, and real estate agents want to deliver that instantly rather than having to go into an office. However, the point upon which most don't agree is to what extent this applies and how best to deliver it. Capitalism at its finest, don't you just love it!

What is fascinating is the level of concern radiating from representatives of the large independent brokerage side of the fence. Cameron Merage is the President & CEO of First Team Real Estate, one of the 20 largest brokerages in the country. Here's what he writes:

More than ever there is an intensified evolving gap between price and value in all aspects of our industry. Whereas in the past, long term relationships between agents and clients on the one hand, and brokerages and their agents on the other, were substantially based on strength of personality, more and more today there is a demand for the delivery of quantifiable value. To compete in the current innovative

economy, just coming up with innovations isn't enough. In fact, there are already plenty of innovative tools available; however it's sorting out the application of the most appropriate innovations in technology, marketing, training, and other areas that counts. What will matter is the leveraging of innovation to create added value in order to stay on the edge of consumer and agents' demand.

Cameron is absolutely on point when he says that real estate used to be about strength of personality. Today, it's about delivering quantifiable value. It's the Jerry Maguirization of real estate: **Don't tell me you love me; just show me the money.**

Similarly we find Gino Blefari of Intero Real Estate Services, another one of the largest brokerages in the country, saying:

The core business model would be set up to help agents run their business more efficiently, effectively, and profitably. The new model will need to have a wealth-building

component that creates collaboration companywide. But this collaboration can't simply be agent-specific or branch-specific; it must be companywide to include a sales executive's ability to financially benefit from all the vertical and horizontal growth of their company.

Gino goes on to outline a new model for the future that involves lead generation, far better training, a better work/life balance for REaltors®, and a focus on philanthropy.

We have in numerous chapters in the last few editions of the *Swanepoel TRENDS Report* written about the evolution of the existing business model and the birth of a variety of new models. Well, this shift continues in a big way and is one of the most significant trends to emerge over the last decade.

Industry leader Realogy, and specifically their respective brand CEOs have reason to be confident—many are featured in this year's Trends Report: Alex Perriello (in this chapter), Budge Huskey (Trend chapter #5), Bruce Zipf (trend chapter #6), Sherry Chris (Trend chapter #7), Phillip

White (Trend chapter #8), and Rick Davidson (Trend chapter #9). Collectively they oversee the largest real estate franchise network in the world, and it is a long uphill road for any company to overtake them (it isn't even close if you combine the brands under Realogy Franchise Group). This would be especially true of a new one attempting to make significant inroads, let alone dethrone them.

But the longstanding classic brands such as Coldwell Banker and Century 21 are not invulnerable; the phenomenal growth of RE/MAX and Keller Williams has shown that innovation and success can be attained, and market share can be had.

that few others are asking. And we're trying to answer them. The more I can get you to think about these scenarios, the more we have succeeded in preparing you for the future.

So the real takeaway for this chapter is not whether large global brands or independents or cloud-based companies will grow the most over the next few years, but for everyone to accept that the value of the real estate brokerage business model itself is under severe pressure as the same technology innovations that allows agents to untether from a physical location at the same time also untethers from the traditional strength-of-personality-based brokerage.

> Remember, we are not delivering judgment about the validity, just asking the strategically tough questions that few others are asking. And we're trying to answer them. The more I can get you to think about these scenarios, the more we have succeeded in preparing you for the future.

So, will future successful models be similar to the eXp and United Real Estate models (CEOs featured in this chapter) or maybe a Redfin, @Properties, or HomeSmart. Only time will tell and, as we have in the past, we'll be there to analyze it and objectively provide you information you can use for your own planning.

Whether or not the physical real estate office completely disappears is yet be seen, but that really isn't the fundamental point. Maybe you should ask yourself, "What is a real estate brokerage really?" Cameron Merage notes that the disconnect between price and value isn't about the personality of the broker, but rather it's about the profitability of the agent. Dan Duffy is trying to bring a hyper low-cost technology based model to the industry. Michael McClure says an agent can do everything out of Starbucks—and he can. So what is the brokerage? What does the broker actually do or have to do? Do agents still have to keep on paying a broker?

Remember, we are not delivering judgment about the validity, just asking the strategically tough questions

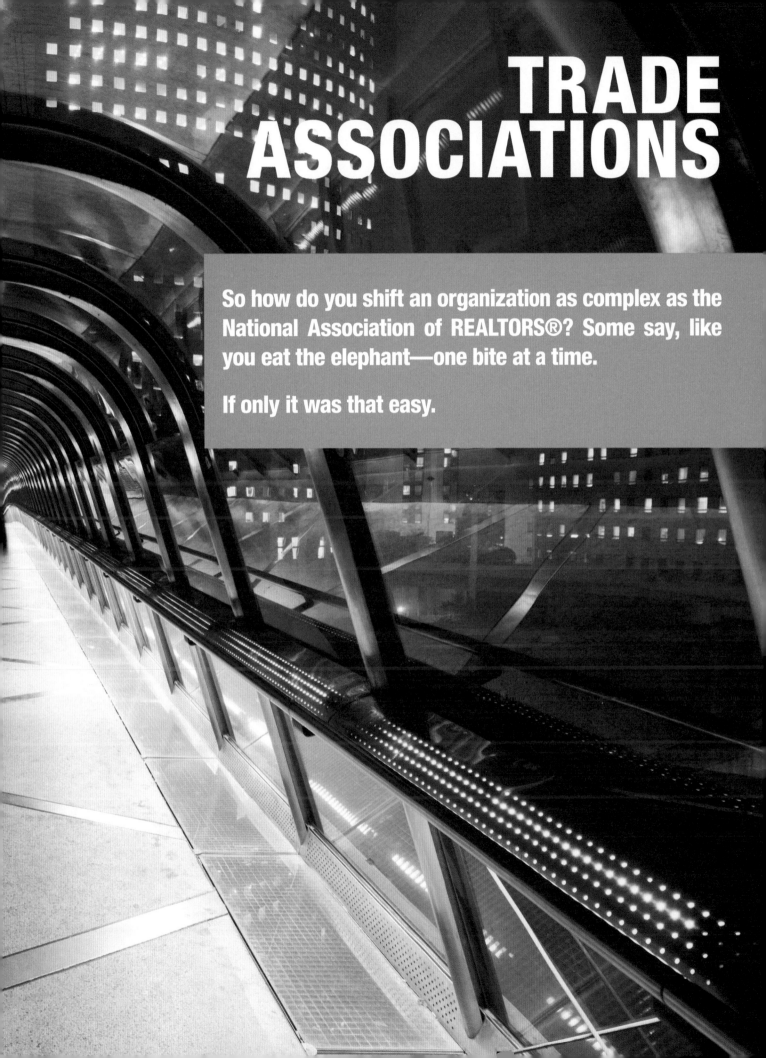

TRADE ASSOCIATIONS

So how do you shift an organization as complex as the National Association of REALTORS®? Some say, like you eat the elephant—one bite at a time.

If only it was that easy.

Trade Associations

The unique three-way agreement tying national to state to local is the envy of many other associations, yet it is also the same structure that causes some big questions. For example, the association is managed, at least in some part, by an oversized Board of Directors comprised of more than 800. Directors that represent Realtors® from all corners of the U.S.; similar to the House of Representatives. That's not a bad thing; it's just very cumbersome, impossible to get everyone on the same page and of course, very costly.

Another historic carryover from yester-year's association structure is the fact that there are some 1,400 REALTOR® associations throughout the country. Again, this is a structure that is the yearning of many, and of course, also enormously powerful. But the viewpoint changes when you grasp that approximately 1,000 of these associations have less than 300 members and the smallest association has less than five. Most are therefore not really economically viable, let alone ready to assume the responsibility of being a change leader.

Add to that that the CEO of the NAR has his hands basically tied behind his back as he can't control them but also doesn't have the authority to close them down. Why? Because they are separately incorporated companies, each with their own charter, goals and board of directors. Creating minimum standards would be a very workable solution but who will step up to the plate to create such guidelines. And furthermore, will leaders step up and be real leaders, which take hard decisions that will significantly reengineer their association? Many say yes, but then don't or can't execute on that statement.

At the state level, with few exceptions, the primary association function has been minimized as a result of the forward and backward expansion of both the national and local associations. That's not a criticism; it's just a result of what has occurred. At each level, the expansion of services has caused overlap and duplication.

Those that have followed my writing will know that not only am I a very optimistic person, I am an avid supporter of organized real estate, especially the REALTOR® Association. I for one believe there are solutions, a purpose, and a value proposition for NAR. So, in an effort to get the issues on the table, we asked several executives to provide us their thoughts and not hold back. Here was the question we posed:

QUESTION

What is the probable course for organized real estate (ORE) over the next three to five years and what role will it play in a new and rapidly evolving and/or transitioning real estate industry.

DALEStinton
CEO - National Association of REALTORS®

I have been asked to opine on the probable course organized real estate will take over the next three to five years, in a rapidly evolving/transitioning real estate industry. There is particular irony in this question, at least from my perch, attempting to dissect what "organized real estate" really means.

The phrase is often used as a shorthand way of referring to the "world of Realtor®" as compared to the rest. To be sure, the differentiation is necessary since there are roughly 2mm plus real estate licensees in this country and at current year-end pace, about 1,050,000 of them are Realtors® (which yes, means they are members of the National Association of REALTORS®). Add to the mix others who more recently have come to appreciate the integrity and value of this time honored, vigorously defended, immediately recognizable brand (such as our friends with the Russian Guild of Realtors, the National Association of Realtors-India, and perhaps the behemoth to the Far East will be next) and the term "organized" begins to take on more meaning.

However, at times I have heard others quick to amend the phrase to "federated", implying a more loosely aligned structure. When things seem to be going well, usually defined as a decent and/or growing market—

distinction drawn between organized and federated is labored and strained, a product of one too many strat planning word smithing sessions. For those who prefer a more direct, less nuanced message, let's be very clear—the

> Let's be very clear—the time is now TO ORGANIZE AS ONE AND COMMIT TO EACH OTHER WITH URGENT RESOLVE.

we're organized, we're like family, and we're tight. When things are dicier or there is tension in the system—we're "federated," like third cousins many times removed.

Some may not be "feeling it", thinking the

time is now TO ORGANIZE AS ONE AND COMMIT TO EACH OTHER WITH URGENT RESOLVE. Current threats to the system (commission-thirsty outsiders, broker/association and broker/MLS chafing, data syndication offenders, insert your favorite here) are real for sure, but they are also symptomatic of the larger problem—we are fractured and becoming more and more fragmented every day. Organized real estate should not be a concept, it's not an ideology, it must be a real, tangible, reliable collective. It was real once, I know this to be true. Where else would the offer of cooperation and compensation have come from? How else could we be celebrating the 100th anniversary of the Code of Ethics, and what about the MLS, the HomeBuilders, RPAC, Realtor.com, and most recently, RPR and the Realtor Party? Organized real estate means room for all but "one" in a common purpose; standing shoulder to shoulder as "one." Moving strategically as "one." Committed to each other as "one." 2014 NAR President Steve Brown's mantra "the time is now" is NOT a slogan; it's a call for action to all.

In my opinion, the opportunity does not require a revolution. Jim Collins observes in his book Great by Choice that, more often than not, organizations become great incrementally. Involved members of times past have celebrated the deliberative processes that almost always brought us to the right decisions, in the right time, and in the right place. More recently though, leadership and members alike have grown impatient to discover a new future, one built on the shoulders of those that came before them, but relevant to the era ahead. All agree, we must move carefully and incrementally, but quickly, with dispatch and purpose, to preserve and protect future generations of Realtors®.

So to the original question in 3-5 years the course we will have taken is this: It will not have been the road less traveled, it will be the road familiar in times gone by when the only thing that mattered was the broker, the agent and their clients. The journey must include Brokers,

Agents, Franchises, Independents, the National, State, and Local Associations, the Institutes, Societies, and Councils, and the MLSs.

An excellent incremental beginning would be to reinvent and strengthen the Three-Way Agreement. We must "raise our own bar" as we ask our members to raise theirs. How can we ask change of our members, without first stepping in to the breach ourselves? We must clearly define the role and responsibilities of the National, State, and Local Associations, removing all duplication, containing costs, and rationalizing our services. We must redefine performance and expectations. Each level should only do what it is best positioned and competent to do. We must once and for all "right size" the organization to an appropriate and sustainable level, and yes, this likely means we will be "smaller," more nimble, more relevant for the times, at ALL three levels. And yes, this too likely means we will be "smaller" in total membership.

If we are to be genuine in our efforts to brand our members as "the top of the food chain in real estate," the much discussed "trusted advisors" in the space, should the system that supports them aspire to anything less for itself? So President Steve Brown is right—the time IS now, change is upon us, let's not act in our own self interest to feel safer or that we've protected our jobs for a few more years. Organized real estate must stand for something much more than that. Returning to our roots reveals our future—strong, professional brokerages, strong professional agents, and strong professional broker/agent relationships, admired and trusted implicitly by an information-saturated consumer who has a right to expect no less.

> It will not have been the road less traveled, it will be the road familiar in times gone by when the only thing that mattered was the broker, the agent and their clients. The journey must include Brokers, Agents, Franchises, Independents, the National, State, and Local Associations, the Institutes, Societies, and Councils, and the MLSs.

BOBMoline

President & COO - HomeServices of America

While it's common to identify organized real estate (ORE) with the NAR (and its state and local associations), I define it more broadly and include title, mortgage, and other real estate related trade organizations, such as the Real Estate Providers Council (RESPRO®), The Realty Alliance, and Association of License Law Officials (ARELLO).

The real estate transaction is often confusing, cumbersome, and complex. So for ORE to be relevant, its value proposition must focus on the overall consumer experience and the critical role that real estate agents play in its delivery. Industry surveys consistently report that buyers and sellers find tremendous value in the convenience and peace of mind in the one-stop shopping concept: full-service teams of professionals all working together to ensure an accurate and on-time closing.

ORE did not change much for 25 years until the advent of technology and increased government involvement in housing policy. However, it still operates in silos focused on their particular agenda. For example, the NAR focuses on real estate brokerage; the American Land Title Association (ALTA) focuses on escrow and title insurance issues, and the Mortgage Bankers Association (MBA) focuses on mortgage lending issues. As a result many times there is dissension among the different silos resulting in differing messages of what is in the consumers' best interest to be delivered to lawmakers and regulators.

The National Association of REALTORS® provides many useful and valuable services to its members today. It sets a standard of professionalism for its membership embodied in its Code of Ethics and Standards of Practice, and along with education has raised the bar for real estate.

The NAR's work on political issues is vital as is its work to foster home ownership through various successful programs. Its economic housing research provides great information for members in their daily marketing of real estate services while their legal arm has assisted members in numerous ways, including patent troll litigation, best practices, real estate forms, and others.

It is my belief that the perceived growing divide between those who strongly support OREs and those who see them as irrelevant, is over blown, not unlike today's polling indicating that Congress is disliked and has to change, yet voters in each election generally send back the same representatives and senators. The dilemma for OREs is whether they deliver relevant services to their members efficiently and cost effectively. For example, during the real estate melt down in 2007/8, most real estate brokers had to dramatically cut costs through downsizing of employees and lease space. The NAR ultimately lost several hundred thousand members and saw a decrease in dues dollars.

However, its various tiers were insulated against having to adapt due to reserves largely created from the multiple listing services. The NAR and the state and local associations are set up as non-for-profits to serve their members while MLSs are normally set up as separate entities owned by the parent association to comply with the tax code. The tax status leads to a disingenuous argument that an MLS is for profit and should compete for revenues and have a mission separate from the associations' mission, which is to serve its member brokers and agents. In today's Internet world these 900plus MLSs are inefficient and in serious need of consolidation. Consolidation of the MLSs into a smaller number of more efficient and larger MLSs, coupled with

on listings and historical sold data that would become the first authority on real estate and would be able to sell information creating revenue to drive down MLS costs for real estate agents.

This site would attract substantial traffic, which would enhance lead generation for the benefit of brokers and agents. The leads would be distributed equitably without additional cost. Corporate governance could preserve the brokers right to decide where their listings are displayed. In summation, all brokers would be allowed to participate and would control the display of their listings, leads would be distributed equitably without cost, costs to provide the MLS could be driven down benefiting real estate agents, and

> They [MLSs] should however, refrain from offering marketing services meant for use in the public arena.

appropriate corporate governance and direction, could save Realtors® several hundred million dollars a year in MLS fees.

In my opinion, MLSs should provide non-marketing services that have almost universal adoption by real estate agents; for example lock boxes, real estate forms, and tax data. They should however, refrain from offering marketing services meant for use in the public arena. If MLSs provide marketing programs/technology to all agents, then no one can differentiate themselves from another. This leads to a less-than optimal adoption rate even though all agents, in some way, are paying for the marketing service. MLSs should consolidate into a smaller, more manageable number and they should act as a data depository and protector of information on listings, sales, and other pertinent real estate data. Brokers could then decide where they wanted their listings displayed and know that the data is properly protected. The elimination of hundreds of MLSs will substantially lower the cost of services and agents and brokers would receive the benefit of lower fees. Failure to address these MLS issues will provide a tempting target for outliers to disintermediate the process.

In a utopian world, there would be one National MLS that would function like a cooperative. The corporate governance would allow for a democratic type structure where all brokers participate. It could provide a public-facing site with a complete set of up-to-date information

consumers would have access to the most up-to-date real estate information available.

The consumer polling is indisputable that reveals that consumers like "one-stop" shopping. We therefore need to embrace a seamless real estate transaction where consumers can shop for services without the inconvenience of having to visit multiple vendors—a consumer-centric market place. Achieving this utopian real estate experience begins with a single trade organization that embraces all the major real estate services required to purchase and close a real estate transaction. For example, the NAR, ALTA, and the MBA would merge into one organization, called for example the National Association of Real Estate Services Providers (NARESP). NARESP would work to overcome the differences between real estate brokerage, escrow/title, and mortgage providers while staying focused on delivering seamless and competitive products to the consumer. NARESP would have greater interaction with Congress, consumer groups, and the regulatory agencies, which should lead to better consumer disclosures and laws. Too often laws or regulations are implemented which actually hurt the consumer with unintended and adverse consequences when they are put into practice. That would be Utopia, but unfortunately the probable course for OREs in the next three to five years, is likely to be more of the same.

DAVID Charron
President & CEO - MRIS

a) The three-way agreement will undergo enormous scrutiny (probably not revision) in the next 36 months. Absent revision, brokers and agents will continue voting with their feet (see South Carolina, Georgia, Washington State and Southern Virginia). Entities representing real estate professionals will continue to define and defend their respective value positions every day. None of us will be immune to calls for "credibility" and "value."

b) Look for the NAR to migrate from its 1.0 million members to one that is a voice representing a potentially smaller "coalition of the willing;" a group that adheres to the positions of the NAR yet distinct from other markets (or entities) that are "not so willing." The NAR

expends loads of cycles applying lubricant to squeaky wheels. Those that repeatedly challenge its positions or whose models vary substantially from templates it provides simply take too much effort with marginal returns.

c) The broker will continue to take steps to regain the high ground with the consumer. This starts by exercising greater influence over and guidance of their managers and agents.

d) Content will still rule. The broker will rein in the "unintended" use of the listing content often experienced as a result of "unattended" syndication. With the market rebounding and the digital environment continuing to evolve, the days of "set it and forget it" are over. Call it smart syndication. Broker brands will experiment with various forms of "co-opetition" to ensure the value of their listing assets are maximized.

e) The MLSs role, serving as steward of the information and traffic cop on an increasingly congested roadway, will be even more challenging. Technology and enforcement will play larger roles to ease the congestion and provide better, more credible information for the benefit of those who will rely on it.

f) MLSs will be competing for the attention and loyalty of the broker and agent. Despite being the default information exchange, factions will form and operate just outside the lines and charter of the MLS. Some of these will be borne out of opportunity; others the result of frustration. Consequently, the rules of engagement will be made and broken concurrently. Effective communication with an increasingly eclectic base will be critical for the MLS.

g) Litigation is the price of success. Regulatory, technology, patent and copyright issues will be front and center. By necessity, industry participants will become more sophisticated on intellectual property and related issues. Costs and impacts to ORE will be significant.

BOBBemis
Founder - Procuring Cause

The most significant trend in the real estate industry that will continue for the next three to five years is really a two-pronged trend. Influence of the consumer and the expectation of younger consumers to have more and more control over and involvement in their real estate purchase process will continue to increase. At the same time the involvement of traditional real estate agents in areas that increasingly do not require either licensure or professional expertise will continue to diminish.

Professional practitioners must concentrate more on those portions of the process that require professional input and trained guidance and experience. The industry will no longer have a place for mere mechanics who can fill out forms, chauffeur buyers, and unlock lockboxes, but who offer little in the way of guidance or experience in those areas of the transaction where such guidance and experience is essential.

This natural selection process will favor those who have prepared early and properly. Those who have garnered the experience necessary will succeed in this evolving real estate model. Agents will no longer be able to learn on the job at the expense of buyers (or sellers) who are as knowledgeable as they are. We will therefore see the introduction and increasing use of apprenticeships in real estate practice. New licensees will acquire the experience necessary to solo, while under the tutelage and guidance of more senior agents. Brokers will have to provide such apprenticeship programs either using experienced working agents or perhaps retired practitioners willing to volunteer the time and effort to train their successors.

As a result, the number of licensed real estate agents, and consequently potential members of the NAR, would drop precipitously. This will bring about a dramatic internal reorganization of the country's largest trade association and will significantly diminish its role in political advocacy.

Consumers will continue to be served and their needs will continue to be met by more numerous and broader-based online service providers. The migration of real estate search away from broker and agent websites to the national real estate portals is just the beginning of this shift.

New entities will emerge to address other underserved segments of the real estate transaction process. This movement will further reduce the menu of services that mechanic agents can offer that the consumer can't acquire on their own. The real estate process is still highly fragmented. Separate services for home inspection, title insurance, closing services, pest certification, appraisal, document management, electronic signatures, escrow services, even potentially open house management, and concierge showing services are all areas that could see new web-based replacement offerings in the years to come. More

the home buying process they will increasingly demand justification for the traditional practice of cooperating commission. Buyers' agents will be hard-pressed to rationalize to a buyer why the agent is paid more in commission if the buyer pays more for the house. Such pressure will eventually bring about the demise of cooperative compensation. When that happens, the core underpinning principle of the multiple listing service will evaporate. That loss of purpose, coupled with increasing facility in direct peer-to-peer sharing of listing data between broker networks, will cause MLSs to dramatically rethink their mission and purpose. They will need to reform themselves into marketing and process management engines if they want to survive.

> This natural selection process will favor those who have prepared early and properly. Those who have garnered the experience necessary will succeed in this evolving real estate model.

momentous will be the combination and aggregation of such services into more complete web-based management systems used equally and cooperatively by agents and consumers alike.

When these new services start to emerge, the anger, fear, and frustration felt by today's agents toward more mundane competition like national listing websites will seem insignificant by comparison.

Such eventualities challenge the current real estate infrastructure to evolve and offer a more complete solution to the professional practitioner or risk becoming even more trite and unnecessary. Given the competition that erupted in late 2013 between brokers and their MLS to define what the proper role of the multiple listing service should be, MLSs will be challenged to map a strategic path that allows real estate practitioners to remain essential to the home buying process. And they will have to accomplish this without encroaching on similar such services the brokers themselves want to offer as a brand differentiator.

As if MLSs didn't have enough to worry about, as consumers become more sophisticated with respect to

The reengineering of the mission of the MLS from facilitator of cooperation, compensation, and data management to provider of process management services will accelerate what up until now has been a laggard effort to consolidate MLS systems into larger cooperatives. While the old adage that "all real estate is local" may continue to hold true, it doesn't necessarily follow that the process by which such purchases are made is equally microcosmic. The reengineering of the real estate process infrastructure will be challenging and costly, and not for the weak of heart or pocketbook. The need for deep pockets to make the investment required will accelerate merger activities at the MLS level and may cause more association consolidates as a collateral effect.

JERRY Matthews

Founder - Jerry Matthews Advisor

In next few years there could be a substantial change in the operating philosophy and structural model of Realtor® Associations. The current association model was created decades ago and has changed very little and its structure is based on two premises: inclusive and passive.

The membership criteria are purposely minimal, as the desire is to have the entire industry under a single organization. The intent is to elevate the business through mass education and communication and therefore the advocacy role demands a large membership in order to have leverage in the political arena through campaign organization and sheer numbers.

The role of the association is to provide access to a set of programs, products, and services absent any responsibility for implementation or proficiency. Effective application is up to the individual agent or broker. This inclusive and passive philosophy defines an organization with no responsibility for the actions or ability of the member. It delivers, and steps aside. It has been my experience that even the best association, operating under a current business model, realizes that a new model could yield much better results. However, a new model demands a dramatically different way of thinking.

The membership criteria for a new association would be purposefully tough, as the desire is to have the success leaders in the profession as members. And a focused definition of the real estate practice would be necessary. Therefore, only a narrow band of practitioners would be sought for membership, resulting in a much smaller total. To be exclusive, the membership criteria must be very high. However, advocacy would not be compromised as those most successful in a profession would participate in far greater numbers in campaigns and political activities, and have more practical influence. The association would aggressively deliver programs, products, and services, but also accept direct responsibility for the actions and capabilities of the members. It would assure compliance and attest to proficiency.

The movement to this new association would require a substantial shift, not only to the premises, but also moving the core programs, products, and services as follows:

- Inclusive to Exclusive
- Passive to Active
- Education to Competency
- Information to Intelligence
- Ethics to Professionalism
- Communications to Connections
- Advocacy to Influence
- Serving the Member to Advancing the Profession

Is it possible with all the changes around us that the Realtor® Association model won't change too? As with the real estate business, the change will probably be driven from outside challengers.

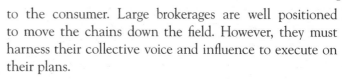

KEVIN McQueen

President - Focus Forward Consulting

Companies grow and prosper by delivering value to people with money. In real estate, those who give consumers what they want will succeed. Organized real estate (ORE) is a complicated mess that is not serving buyers and sellers. It's not nimble it wasn't built to be. And it's no surprise that the value and innovation are coming from outside.

Large brokerages represent one segment of ORE that will likely prosper. They have the necessary capital, scale, intelligence, and relevancy. They will not be alone as some small niche brokerages and solid high-production agents will navigate this as well. Savvy brokerages are cutting their deals now, while many others are constantly complaining about the wrong things and trying to protect their cheese. The key to survival and success is the delivery of value

to the consumer. Large brokerages are well positioned to move the chains down the field. However, they must harness their collective voice and influence to execute on their plans.

At the greatest risk in ORE are the 83 percent of local Realtor® Associations, with less than 1,000 members each. These 1,173 associations (out of 1,400) won't exist in 2018. This is because the vast majority of the members and brokerage decision-makers don't get sufficient value from the locals, other than MLS. Most members don't support the three-way agreement, so the NAR and the state associations are at risk as well. When Realtor® membership is no longer tied to MLS; the pace of change will greatly accelerate.

MLS is valued. There are four legs to the MLS stool: data, technology, an organized marketplace, and a means of getting paid. Data and technology are not local and they never were. And 900 MLSs are simply unsustainable. If 80 percent of the associations go away, the smallest MLSs will either merge or disappear. The smart ones are making their moves right now. Consolidation is slowly taking place—three new regional MLSs were formed in 2013 (26 MLSs working together resulting in 3 regionals). Brokers will continue to demand more of this, resulting in greater efficiency and eventually, less than 200 well-run MLS providers will remain. In three years, brokers will own a bigger market share of the remaining MLSs and most will be broker controlled.

In conclusion, large brokerages are the ones who will lead this substantial shift. We call it the OREO Movement (organized real estate opportunity). These brokerages, along with their allies already know they don't need 1,400 local association chapters or 900 different and separate data and technology providers (MLSs). The current infrastructure can't deliver what consumers and brokers need. The OREO Movement is upon us now, and it will be an exciting ride with a lot of consolidation over the next three to five years.

> At the greatest risk... are the 83 percent of local Realtor® Associations, with less than 1,000 members each.

JEREMYCONAWAY

President - RECON Intelligence Services

Any discussion regarding the mid-term role of organized real estate (ORE) must start with a quick look at its present status and current dynamic.

In this case that task was made easier by the fact that the preparation of this piece was started in San Francisco even as the NAR was winding up its 2013 annual meetings. The annual meetings, perhaps better than any other event, reflect the personality and temperament of an organization of nearly 20,000 individuals that all have one thing in common. Some attendees are Realtor® politicians there to seek higher office within the Realtor® culture and others are Ribbonites that are easy to spot because of the bright colored ribbons on which they proclaim their current status within the organization. Then there are those that have come to learn from any one of the dozens of classes, presentations, forums, and the trade show where scores of

vendors peddle their wares as a key part of this $60 billion plus industry. Finally there are those who are just there to collect on their semi-annual, all expenses paid travel reward for services rendered at the local and state levels. And all of these attendees will probably receive that which they sought, and within this simple quid pro quo can be found the commanding dynamic of the organization. But what one won't find at the annual meeting are demonstrators, protesters, dissenters, revolutionaries, or counter culture types because the system has long fulfilled its promise to take care of its loyal and committed patrons.

Yet, this observation has been made frequently over the past twenty-five years with little or no effect. A prime example of this predictive dysfunction is the NAR governance process. It is totally irrelevant in terms of contemporary governance design. However, it's more than adequate as a beloved, historic relic and reward system as evidenced by another constituency that sings for the status quo; ORE's several thousand employees. From AE's to clerks, they all appear to be comfortable with life as they know it.

The sheer size of ORE defies meaningful re-engineering or reconfiguration absent a major crisis. It's like the giant ocean tanker quietly passing through the Harbor. Its momentum alone would carry it for several years before anyone would take note of a need to change. And therein lies ORE's strength and relative satisfaction.

A similar analysis can also be used to describe what can be found at both the state and local levels. Hundreds of local REALTOR® Associations have less than 100 members with staff and support structures that are essentially overwhelmed by obsolescence and a lack

appear to be already moving in that direction by simply dropping their Realtor® memberships. However, there is at least one sanctioned effort to move ORE at a rate greater than its hull speed. At the current time organized real estate is tolerating a strategic planning alternative appropriately call REThink. During several dozen presentations over the past two years in all corners of the Realtor® domestic world these would-be progressives have joined in a reasonably creative but carefully facilitated process. Neither can one overlook the fact the ORE is also sponsoring a wide range of creative and innovative projects, some through the NAR's 2nd Century Initiatives.

If the right conditions were to occur, is there a more relevant and innovative role for organized real estate to play? Absolutely. Many of the business and

> The sheer size of ORE defies meaningful re-engineering or reconfiguration absent a major crisis.

of resources. But, those 100 are happy. Even appropriately sized large local REALTOR® Associations currently find themselves awash in the wake of their own legacies, irrelevance, and declining numbers of committed members. Lost in all this is the fact that the same ORE member who refuses to pay another twenty dollars in dues is now more than willing to pay Zillow $240 per month.

The state REALTOR® Association structure is similarly configured. With perhaps two or three exceptions, the primary function of a state association has been reduced to being a conduit transporting committed Realtor® volunteers from local to national functions. Their signature task is government relations, a function that some suggest could be handled by a vendor at a fraction of the cost.

Neither is there any apparent enlightenment or inspiration to be gained from examining other major professional associations; the American Medical Association, the American Dental Association, or the American Bar Association have all seen both their membership and influence fall to historic lows.

Is there a possibility that progressive forces will stage a coup? Probably not. The trailing Boomers are focused on achieving a survivable retirement. If Generations X and Y Realtors® want to move in a different direction, all they have to do is to start a new Realtor® movement. And some

professional challenges being faced by the industry today could be positively impacted through a united and multi-generational coalition of engaged and committed ORE members. But that won't happen until those that are content with the status quo see the need and join the vision. As a result, for the next three to five years, control of ORE is likely to remain in the hands of its committed Civic and Boomer members. They have earned this right, it is their association, and whatever they decide will mark the course.

What role will ORE play in the rapidly changing real estate industry? It won't be a wave flying out from the bow, a flag signaling from the mast, or a snapping spinnaker straining at its pole. It will continue to play its timeless role as the industry's keel. Maintaining stability, balance, and steerage is a good and necessary thing. Providing a stable platform for those who wish to thrill themselves by leaning out over the rushing water is an important contribution. Those who find this situation to be unacceptable might opt for a tour of local restaurants in San Francisco—lots of happy faces there.

SUMMARY, Opinion and Take Away

We have discussed ORE numerous times previously and specifically in both the 2012 and 2013 editions of the *Swanepoel TRENDS Report*. It is evident from the contributions in this chapter that the fork in the road is dead ahead.

Organized Real Estate (ORE) as we know it has been in existence for over a hundred years and has contributed more to the overall value proposition of being a real estate professional than any other single group.

So let's begin with the most important voice in organized real estate, and probably the most significant CEO the NAR has ever had, that of Dale Stinton. Dale's position is mostly upbeat and positive, but one cannot help but detect something else. His statement could be described as an appeal rather than a prediction; it is exhortatory, not explanatory. He says (emphasis mine):

For those who prefer a more direct, less nuanced message, let's be very clear—the time is now TO ORGANIZE AS ONE AND COMMIT TO EACH OTHER WITH URGENT RESOLVE. Current threats to the system (commission-thirsty outsiders, broker/association and broker/MLS chafing, data syndication offenders, insert your favorite here) are real for sure, but they are also symptomatic of the larger problem—we are fractured and becoming more and more fragmented every day. Organized real estate should not be a concept, it's not an ideology, it must be a real, tangible, reliable collective. It was real once, I know this to be true.

Those are not words filled with confidence because there is good reason for urgency of resolve.

David Charron, the CEO of MRIS, is one of the wise men of organized real estate, with decades of experience with both MLSs and associations. He is predicting pressure on the Three Way Agreement that binds the local, state, and national associations together, and a NAR that is no longer a million members strong, but a "voice representing a coalition of the willing." David also sees immense pressure on the MLS to retain the loyalty of its brokers, especially urgent in light of recent developments between the largest brokerages and the NAR-governed MLS system as a whole.

Bob Moline, the President of HomeServices of America, and one of the leaders in the movement by large brokerages to redefine the relationship between brokerages and organized real estate, clarifies the reason. The MLS is doing too much marketing:

In my opinion, MLSs should provide non-marketing services that have almost universal adoption by real estate agents; for example lock boxes, real estate forms, and tax data. They should however, refrain from offering marketing services meant for use in the public arena. If MLSs provide marketing programs/technology to all agents, then no one can differentiate himself from another. This leads to a less-than optimal adoption rate even though all agents, in some way, are paying for the marketing service.

He also advocates for MLS consolidation, suggesting that the ideal state would be one national MLS for all brokers. Once again, one is struck by how Bob's response to my question isn't so much of a prediction as it is a prescription; it is more about what the industry should do rather than what the industry will do. I was impressed by his contribution.

A similar viewpoint is echoed by Jerry Matthews as he advocates for a new association for a new age that turns the existing understanding on its head. As he succinctly puts it:

The movement to this new association would require a substantial shift, not only to the premises, but also moving the core programs, products, and services as follows:

- *Inclusive to Exclusive*
- *Passive to Active*
- *Education to Competency*
- *Information to Intelligence*
- *Ethics to Professionalism*
- *Communications to Connections*
- *Advocacy to Influence*
- *Serving the Member to Advancing the Profession*

Is it possible with all the changes around us that the Realtor® Association model won't change too?

The future, we hope, will see the Realtor® model change, and drastically. But once again, this is not prediction, it's more a call to action.

Perhaps the reason for so much preaching is that thinking about what the industry will do instead of what it should do induces despair. Bob Bemis, the former CEO of ARMLS and VP at Zillow, who has seen all of the sides in the current real estate landscape, does engage in prediction. And it is nothing short of a doomsday scenario for organized real estate:

As if MLSs didn't have enough to worry about, as consumers become more sophisticated with respect to the home buying process they will increasingly demand justification for the traditional practice of cooperating commission. Buyers' agents will be hard-pressed to rationalize to a buyer why the agent is paid more in commission if the buyer pays more for the house. Such pressure will eventually bring about the demise of cooperative compensation.

As he points out, without cooperation and compensation, the raison d'être of the MLS disappears. And without the MLS, Charron's vision of the much smaller "coalition of the willing" is far more likely than Stinton's appeal for greater unity.

One could disagree with Bob's prediction about the demise of cooperation and compensation, but not a single leader we consulted thinks the status quo can be maintained. The big trend in the association world, at least if we look at the hopes and dreams of the industry, is consolidation.

Every single Thought Leader spoke of the need for consolidation, and none more straightforwardly than Kevin McQueen, who has been working on precisely that for the past couple of years:

And 900 MLSs are simply unsustainable. If 80 percent of the associations go away, the smallest MLSs will either merge or disappear. The smart ones are making their moves right now. Consolidation is slowly taking place—three new regional MLSs were formed in 2013 (26 MLSs working together resulting in 3 regionals). Brokers will continue to demand more of this, resulting in greater efficiency and eventually, less than 200 well-run MLS providers will remain. In three years, brokers will own a bigger market share of the remaining MLSs and most will be broker controlled.

Should it come to pass, none of the leaders we spoke with would shed a tear. Even Dale Stinton has publicly supported consolidation, particularly of small local associations. That is not to say that no one would shed a tear if consolidation should occur. One of the most realistic, if not depressing, takes comes from Jeremy Conaway, a longtime thought leader in organized real estate. He describes the recent NAR Annual Meetings in San Francisco as follows:

The annual meetings, perhaps better than any other event, reflect the personality and temperament of an organization of nearly 20,000 individuals that all have one thing in common. Some attendees are Realtor® politicians there to seek higher office within the Realtor® culture and others are Ribbonites that are easy to spot because of the bright colored ribbons on which they proclaim their current status within the organization. Then there are those that have come to learn from any one of the dozens of classes, presentations, forums, and the trade show where scores of vendors peddle their wares as a key part of this $60 billion plus industry. Finally there are those who are just there to collect on their semi-annual, all expenses paid travel reward for services rendered at the local and state levels. And all of these attendees will probably receive that which they sought, and within this simple quid pro quo can be found the commanding dynamic of the organization. But what one won't find at the annual meeting are demonstrators, protesters, dissenters, revolutionaries, or counter culture types because the system has long fulfilled its

promise to take care of its loyal and committed patrons.

He points out that while hundreds of local associations have fewer than 100 members, they still have staff and support structures that simply cannot do much of anything to keep those 100 members happy. He notes that while the NAR—by extension most state and local Realtor® Associations as well—governance is "totally irrelevant in terms of contemporary governance design," the several thousand employees from Association CEO's to administrative assistants are all "comfortable with life as they know it." Could things change? Jeremy's skeptical:

Is there a possibility that progressive forces will stage a coup? Probably not. The trailing Boomers are focused on achieving a survivable retirement. If Generations X and Y Realtor® want to move in a different direction, all they have to do is to start a new Realtor® movement. And some appear to be already moving in that direction by simply dropping their Realtor® memberships.

One could say he's overly cynical, or that he's simply being realistic. Drawing the strands together, here's what we see happening to organized real estate over the next few years. The warning signs and the dissatisfaction with the status quo from the very top to the very bottom are simply too numerous.

The trend towards consolidation will accelerate; at least if by "accelerate" we mean the effort of a snail going from 1 inch per hour to 1.5 inches per hour. It's a fact that real estate always moves slowly, incrementally. We are with Conaway and Stinton on that point: the pace of change will be glacial. It may not be fast enough, and frankly, it may require that an entire generation of Realtors® and Association leaders pass on to wonderfully manicured golf courses in Paradise Valley, AZ or in Paradise.

But change is coming, because the tensions between Associations, MLS, and the Brokerage communities are now plain, obvious, and building to a critical point.

The breaking point will come between the MLS and large brokerages first, as that tension is the highest today and it most directly impacts the day-to-day business of brokers and agents. That break will then lead to a decrease in membership numbers, particularly for embattled small local associations that have less and less reason to exist without the MLS. And that in turn will trigger more and more consolidation amongst both the MLSs and the associations.

However, this transition will not be smooth and it won't be easy. Those thousands of employees of organized real estate and their supporters who are happy with the status quo who make up so much of the world of the MLS and associations are not going to simply give up without a fight.

We predict, therefore, that while consolidation is the hope and the trend, over the next few years we might see the reverse take place as more and more local associations leave regional MLSs or larger associations and setup their own small MLS. The technology is widely available and inexpensive, and local associations know that their value is access to the MLS. Even as large brokerages push for more and more consolidation, real estate is very much a long-tail fragmented industry, and the smaller brokers (in numbers) can and will fight against the local MLS level.

Contra Jerry Matthews, we don't see the emergence of a new association of real estate professionals. That has been the dream of a generation or more of brokers and agents, but much like the much-hoped-for and much-predicted emergence of a third party in American politics, we'll have to see it to believe it. Far more likely is reform from within organized real estate, either brought on by driven leaders who see that they have to make those changes or perish, or by external circumstances that leave no other options.

Long live the Realtor®.

"Power is an elusive concept."

See the 2013 List

of the 200 Most

Powerful People

in Residential

Real Estate

SWANEPOEL

Power200

SP200.COM

BRANDING

Over the past five years the portals have enjoyed remarkable growth and they are now redefining consumer awareness. Is this the beginning of a huge brand war or is it an extraneous squabble?

Branding

The amazing progress of the aggregators or portals; Zillow, Trulia and Realtor.com, have now placed them in many cases as the first interaction with the home buying public. While these companies and websites aren't real estate brokerage companies, and all have stated that they have no intention to become, they still do provide home buying information to the consumer. So the lines between what they do, and what a broker/agent does, is most certainly becoming blurred – at least from users point of view, if not from the industry's point of view.

When the participants in the real estate industry—the brokers and agents—talk about the most recognizable brand in the home buying process they usually refer to one of the large and well known franchise brands; usually RE/MAX, Century 21, Coldwell Banker or a largest local brokerage a company.

In contrast to the portals, there are very few real estate companies/brands that continually spend significant dollars on corporate branding and identity. And as a result, the portal brands appear to be rapidly gaining consumer awareness as it relates to the home buying process.

Today's online consumer ultimately ends up with (at least for the foreseeable future) a brokerage brand and agent brand when they end up in transaction mode. But is this line being increasingly blurred and one has to wonder whether in three to five years will we find ourselves in a situation where the consumer can no longer distinguish between a website "real estate brand" and an broker/agent "real estate brand." With that as framework we asked some industry "Thought Leaders" to ponder the following:

QUESTION

In your opinion, will the fundamental shift in the home searching process caused by the Internet result in portals becoming a more recognizable brand with the consumer than the large real estate franchise brands.

DAVELiniger
Co-founder & Chairman - RE/MAX

Web portals such as Zillow and Trulia have attracted a great deal of attention in recent years. That attention is well-deserved, because these sites do a good job helping agents promote listings and consumers find properties.

To a large degree, they do what newspaper real estate sections used to do: advertise listings and generate leads for agents.

What they don't do, however, is provide the actual service involved in buying or selling a home. Portals can't replace real estate agents, because although people look for houses on the Internet, they don't buy them there. This isn't like buying a book on amazon.com, and it never will be. A real estate sale is a complex proposition, and people still want a professional—a real live human—to guide them through it. The challenging market of the past few years reinforced the need for professional assistance.

It's worth noting that the question implies that the portals operate in the same segment/industry as the national real estate brands. They don't. They're in the marketing business, with a successful model that provides free consumer access and relies on the listings, cooperation, and advertising dollars of agents and brokerages. If the portals ever tried to move into the brokerage business, they'd destroy their model by alienating the advertisers who create their revenue.

Just as travel websites promote, support, and coexist with hotel and airline brands, entities like Zillow and Trulia are valuable contributors in the real estate ecosystem. They add tremendous efficiency to the process, and their technology serves the interest of consumers and agents alike.

That said, the portals are limited in terms of their emotional impact on consumers. A real estate agent, however, becomes a trusted adviser and even a friend. Multiply that effect hundreds of thousands of times each year and you start to realize why people still think of real estate agents, and their brands, more than a website used along the way.

At its core, real estate remains a business built on relationships. The portals are a fantastic resource, but in the end a real person—someone you come to know and trust—helps you achieve your goals. The name of that person, and the brand he or she represents, is something you remember long after the experience is over.

BUDGEHuskey

President & CEO - Coldwell Banker Real Estate

The answer to this progressively complex question is somewhat opaque... that being both yes and no. Based on current traffic levels to the largest portals, it is impossible to deny their impact on real estate search and the growing distance from all other real estate related sites in terms of visits.

The value of being positioned as an unbiased, third-party source of information is undeniable, and portals have been rewarded accordingly with eyeballs for their buyer-centric design. In addition, within the last year significant advertising and public relations investments have raised brand awareness for the portals to the point where they may now arguably be eclipsing the National Association of REALTORS® as consumer sources of real

estate information and content in the media (even if that content originates from others). So, in the context of the above, the answer must be a resounding yes!

On the other hand, there is an emerging search pattern that is evidenced by an astounding number of reported visits across real estate websites on an aggregated basis as compared to total home sale sides in the U.S. Consumers are clearly not limiting their search to one site, but rather appear to be employing a "funnel" approach where they skim the surface by using various portals in their initial search and then move on to franchise and local company sites for additional detail. The increased level of data timeliness, accuracy, specific property, and community content renders franchise and/or local company sites more valuable to buyers the closer they are to a decision. This assumption appears to be supported by extensive research on leads from across the spectrum, which reflects a higher probability of conversion and therefore overall quality, from the latter. So, based on the above, the answer must be a resounding no!

Regardless of one's position on the real estate portals, a valid conversation is occurring about whether or

> *The historic swim lanes in the real estate pool are incresingly being ignored as others jump in.*

not they have moved beyond the simple premise of online classified advertising into areas claimed by the brokerage or franchise community, as well as how their revenue models will evolve to meet growing investor demands.

The historic swim lanes in the real estate pool are increasingly being ignored as others jump in. But for the moment, one need not view the online presence as merely as a zero sum game with winners and losers. Rather it should be viewed through a prism of complementary positions within the online space in which all will be forced to constantly deliver a more robust, accurate, and compelling consumer experience to be relevant in a future conversation.

Consumer recognition of brands, however, shouldn't be narrowly limited to the online space as there are multiple ways in which impressions are delivered. Yes, the web's influence is unquestionable but one shouldn't discount the impact of other forms of identification such as yard signs, alternative media, community involvement and, most importantly, the people who represent a brand or operating company. Search is only the beginning of a successful real estate transaction. In the end, the most meaningful impression of a real estate brand comes from the professionals within our network who deliver all the aspects comprising an exceptional customer experience. And, in my opinion, an exceptional customer experience is the ultimate competitive advantage in real estate

HAROLDCrye
President & CEO - Crye-Leike Real Estate Services

The internet has had a tremendous impact on the way consumers search for real estate. The real estate industry should be congratulated for making a relatively rapid transition away from traditional print advertising to the internet.

Large independents and franchises CAN compete with national portals within their market area. However, they have a harder time competing on a national basis with the large portals. They must have quality websites that are easy to find, easy to use, quick response times, and provide fresh, accurate data. The local entities are better positioned to do this, plus provide more hyper-local content data and back it up with great customer service like immediate response teams.

The portals don't have the same mission as the local entities, so the well funded ones can move with a single purpose to gain brand recognition without having to deal with the myriad of day-to-day issues of brokerage. They are dependent on brokers for listing content. Early on, most brokers freely gave their listing data to the portals and considered it to be free advertising. Most of them saw this as a way to finally reduce their newspaper advertising expense.

However, the brokerage community is now beginning to realize that it may not be in their best interest to freely give this valuable listing data to the outside portals. Currently there is significant pushback developing. More "black holes" are occurring where the portals don't have all the active listings but the local brokers do. And MLSs are switching to "opt-in" to the portals vs. "opt-out" as they realize that the non-industry players are getting between their agent and the consumer.

Home buying consumers want to see the entire inventory but they still have to engage a trusted, knowledgeable agent and broker on a local level to accomplish their buying or selling objective. Large independents already fare well in their markets with page views and time spent on the site after the consumer has browsed the Internet mainly to see pictures. They will be there when the consumer is searching for the freshest, most accurate property information.

Yes, the portals have become very recognizable brand names but may struggle to remain relevant in the future if they have too many "black holes" in their markets. In that situation, the large local broker and franchise are in a much stronger position

More black holes are occurring...

EARLLee
CEO - HSF Affiliates

Web portals such as Zillow and Trulia have attracted a great deal of attention in recent years. That attention is well-deserved, because these sites do a good job helping agents promote listings and consumers find properties.

and advertising dollars of agents and brokerages. If the portals ever tried to move into the brokerage business, they'd destroy their model by alienating the advertisers who create their revenue.

Just as travel websites promote, support, and coexist with hotel and airline brands, entities like Zillow and Trulia are valuable contributors in the real estate

> Portals will only become more relevant than real estate brokerage brands if we let them.

To a large degree, they do what newspaper real estate sections used to do: advertise listings and generate leads for agents. What they don't do, however, is provide the actual service involved in buying or selling a home. Portals can't replace real estate agents, because although people look for houses on the Internet, they don't buy them there. This isn't like buying a book on amazon.com, and it never will be. A real estate sale is a complex proposition, and people still want a professional—a real live human—to guide them through it. The challenging market of the past few years reinforced the need for professional assistance.

It's worth noting that the question implies that the portals operate in the same segment/industry as the national real estate brands. They don't. They're in the marketing business, with a successful model that provides free consumer access and relies on the listings, cooperation,

ecosystem. They add tremendous efficiency to the process, and their technology serves the interest of consumers and agents alike.

That said, the portals are limited in terms of their emotional impact on consumers. A real estate agent, however, becomes a trusted adviser and even a friend. Multiply that effect hundreds of thousands of times each year and you start to realize why people still think of real estate agents, and their brands, more than a website used along the way.

At its core, real estate remains a business built on relationships. The portals are a fantastic resource, but in the end a real person—someone you come to know and trust—helps you achieve your goals. The name of that person, and the brand he or she represents, is something you remember long after the experience is over.

PAT Riley
President & COO - Allen Tate Companies

BOB Goldberg
SVP - National Association of REALTORS®

"Without a national/international website, you're out of the game" the CEO of HomeServices of America once said.

Yes, Zillow has trumped Realtor.com as the source for real estate data. If you're talking about brand recognition, (even if you have all the data and it is precise), it takes marketing dollars. Geico is living proof. Brand recognition with an income stream to back it up is what it really takes.

Zillow, Trulia and Realtor.com don't have precise, accurate data and are really attracting that 12-18 percent of out-of-marketplace buyers. As long as they don't have all the IDX or syndicated data, once a visitor visits the local marketplace, the buying public will make their own decision on the source of online information as well as Realtor® partner. When it gets to the region, the local MLS public-facing website and the individual Realtor® website takes over because of accuracy and timeliness of the data. Often times, it will then come down to the local market share of the firms, their reputation, and number of yard signs. I still believe whoever controls the listings will control the marketplace. For the 80 percent of buyers who are familiar with their marketplace, the local brand rules. I fear the local MLS sites more than the national because they are initially perceived to have all the info and not the individual broker, which is a false perception. While the syndication sites can out brand and market the broker, the broker data is the more accurate data and the consumer finds that out fast.

With the majority of consumers beginning their home search online, real estate professionals are at a loss if they don't have adequate representation in the space.

And while many currently brand themselves successfully, consumers may not know how to accurately distinguish between those that are real estate agents and those that are Realtors®. In an attempt to stay ahead of this fundamental shift and provide added value to our members, the National Association of REALTORS® is working with the Internet Corporation for Assigned Names and Numbers (ICANN) to secure a new .REALTOR top level domain. The Internet is evolving. Everyone is familiar with domains like dot com, dot org and dot net, and soon thousands of top level domains will be appearing on the Internet. Only members of the NAR and the Canadian Real Estate Association (CREA) will be able to use the .REALTOR domain in connection with their names, making it the trusted source in real estate. According to the NAR's 2013 *Profile of Home Buyers & Sellers*, 92 percent of consumers utilized the Internet in their search. While franchises and brands will continue to be present on the Internet, consumers who come across a .REALTOR domain will immediately know that they are dealing with a Realtor®, a credible, trusted real estate professional that adheres to a strict code of ethics. Our goal is to not only support existing brokerages but to help them by enabling them to leverage the power of the REALTOR® brand. The new .REALTOR domain will be available for registration to Realtor® members (agents and brokers); local and state Realtor® associations; association multiple listing services; affiliated institutes, societies and councils; and other NAR-approved licensees. By getting a head start on the process on behalf oour members, we hope to further differentiate the new .REALTOR domain from all others and in doing so help our members better serve consumers in the future.

MARKAllen

CEO - 10K Research and Marketing

Select portals have captured the attention of the public but I do not think the portals have become a more recognizable brand than the national franchise brands.

Nor do I see them as a lesser second cousin. Both the portals and the real estate franchise brands appear to equally evident to American consumers. The portals are seen by consumers as an independent unbiased source with no stake in persuading the consumer to a particular course of action. Consumers value the unfettered access and appreciate the opportunity to begin their journey in an anonymous fashion. From the consumer perspective, the portals appear to provide initial information resources and tools that inspire consumers to come back for more. Consumers appear to value this whether they are participating out of simple curiosity or beginning a more serious learning curve.

Brokers large and small and the agents who represent them are ever-present at the local level. Their signs abound in yards, billboards, grocery bags and even bathroom walls. Their ads are heard and seen on radio and TV. They are present at cocktail parties and attending youth hockey games. They are committed to school boards, church boards, city boards and charitable boards. Brokers and their agents are the community, the local expert on the local market. Research reflects that consumers rely on them for advice and counsel. Consumers depend on their Realtor® to identify the best resources and trust Realtors® to look out for their best interest in what they readily see is a very complex landscape. I believe the portals help consumers to recognize the complexities that exist in the real estate landscape.

As consumers more fully activate their home buying or selling venture, as they transition from being anonymous to engaging a professional for the assistance they need, they quickly become immersed in the services their broker offers. It is at this point they often become fully aware

the broker has better, more current, more accurate and more complete information on homes for sale and homes sold. It is here the consumer more fully recognizes the value the broker website has to offer. This is supported by an agent who demonstrates a deeper and more personal knowledge of all the intricacies of the local aspect of the

> I believe the portals help consumers to recognize the complexities that exist in the real estate landscape.

neighborhoods the consumer desires. Consumers have demonstrated a keen interest and engagement in what the portals have to offer and the portals have caused some disintermediation in lead generation. But the portals have not displaced the value of the broker brand, including the importance of the broker's information services at the regional level.

SUMMARY, Opinion and Take Away

Based on the responses, when it comes to the big portals, real estate executives all agree that they are very important, but apparently limited and cannot replace the human touch and expertise that the real estate agent contributes.

Dave Liniger, entrepreneur extraordinaire and RE/MAX's founder and driving force, sums it up nicely when he says:

What they don't do, however, is provide the actual service involved in buying or selling a home. Portals can't replace real estate agents, because although people look for houses on the Internet, they don't buy them there.

Many of the other Thought Leaders who also provided commentary for this question agree as they certainly echoed the majority opinion of other Brokerage Leaders.

It's interesting that none of the portals have suggested that they are anything other than a source of information and have publically stated that they don't wish to compete with the services offered by a real estate brokerage company. As a matter of fact, when its acquisition of Market Leader gave Trulia ownership over RealEstate.com with its brokerage licenses, Trulia's leadership was quick to announce that they plan on doing nothing whatsoever with those brokerage licenses, and will get rid of them as if they were radioactive hazards.

The question we asked wasn't whether the big portals—and really, we're talking about Zillow and Trulia as Realtor.com is already a generic kind of a brand—would replace the real estate agent, but whether the portals would become a more recognizable brand with consumers than large brokerage and franchise brands.

This is a very far-reaching question and I believe it elucidates a fundamental shift that is taking place that will have far reaching implications. But let's dial back for a second.

In late 2012 Zillow embarked on its big brand advertising push, initially as a test. Spencer Rascoff talked about that in early 2013:

So we've actually done extensive consumer research in the U.S. and if you ask Americans to name an online real estate website, more people say I don't know or I can't name one than say Zillow, and we're the number one site in the category. And more people say Amazon, that doesn't even have a real estate section at their website, than say the company that's number two in the category.

So just to paint a picture to you by what I mean by brand whitespace, we believe that by advertising and by continuing to invest in product development, we have an opportunity to create a massive enduring brand from which significant shareholder value breaking and margin expansion comes.

So Zillow embarked on a brand advertising campaign in earnest in 2013. The results were so encouraging that Zillow dramatically increased its spending on direct-to-consumer advertising throughout 2013. In Q1, they spent $11.5 million more on sales and marketing year-over-year, and though management didn't break out how much of that was for advertising, they did say most of that increase was due to increased advertising. In Q2 and Q3, Zillow spent $8.4 million and $10.1 million more on advertising respectively. Q4 numbers had not yet been released but they estimate that in 2013 they spent somewhere around $30 million just on consumer brand advertising.

There is no sign that Zillow will slow down in 2014. On the current path, I believe that within five years Zillow will be synonymous with "real estate" the way that Amazon has become synonymous with "online shopping" and Yelp has become synonymous with "local search." Most of the national real estate franchise brands do no significant national corporate advertising/branding, and the previously dominant franchise marketers like RE/MAX have also scaled back dramatically (maybe their recent IPO will lead to increased change that for 2014).

So, while homebuyers/sellers rate the agent that assisted them with a transaction fairly highly, "real estate agents" as a collective have always received a weak report card from the general media. Survey after survey has ranked real estate agents low on the trust list. Real estate companies appear to be even less important or memorable and few home buying consumers appear to have any loyalty toward a specific company or brand.

The simple fact that Trulia and Zillow have grown to become the behemoths they are today at a time when Realtor.com was already the dominant T-Rex and Realtors® basically had a lock on MLS and other real estate data, is mind-boggling.

The trend line is clear. The portals will become a more powerful brand with consumers than brokerages and franchises are. What's more, they will become a more powerful brand with the real estate agent than brokerages and franchises. And there is another hidden potential disruption. The effect of the branding play by the major portals isn't to disrupt the consumer-to-agent relationship; the portals themselves know they can't bring the human touch and help buyers and sellers need to complete the transaction. The effect of the branding play is to disrupt the agent-to-broker relationship, which is fragile to begin with.

Of course he follows that up immediately with, *Consumers are clearly not limiting their search to one site, but rather appear to be employing a "funnel" approach where they skim the surface by using various portals in their initial search and then move on to franchise and local company sites for additional detail.* This echoes Harold Crye's view that large independent brokerages do well in their local markets with page views and time spent on the site.

So the most significant trend we have to acknowledge here—if even begrudgingly—is that if you are a real estate franchise, broker, or agent, the portals have already won the battle for home buying consumer attention and awareness.

Now the next battle will determine if the portals can become more relevant than real estate brokers and agents.

> The trend line is clear. The portals will become a more powerful brand with consumers than brokerages and franchises are.

So we applaud Budge Huskey, CEO of the oldest and one of the most widely respected real estate brands, when he says:

Based on current traffic levels to the largest portals, it is impossible to deny their impact on real estate search and the growing distance from all other real estate related sites in terms of visits. The value of being positioned as an unbiased, third-party source of information is undeniable, and portals have been rewarded accordingly with eyeballs for their buyer-centric design. In addition, within the last year significant advertising and public relations investments have raised brand awareness for the portals to the point where they may now arguably be eclipsing the National Association of REALTORS® as consumer sources of real estate information and content in the media (even if that content originates from others). So, in the context of the above, the answer must be a resounding yes!

I really like what Earl Lee, CEO of the new Berkshire Hathaway HomeServices brand (the first new national real estate franchise brand created in almost a decade), says:

Will the portals, with access to data and consumers, become more relevant than the real estate business and real estate brands? The answer: only if we let them.

Only if we let them!

SWANEPOEL T3 Summit™

LAS VEGAS 2014

APRIL 9 – 11

Program Highlights

- Must-see, in-depth interviews with legendary industry-leading CEOs
- TED-like Talks on some of the industry's most compelling topics
- Thought Leader Panels with key industry thinkers
- Stefan Swanepoel's "What's Coming Next" original Keynote

A few who shared their wisdom in 2013

Ron Peltier
CEO Berkshire Hathaway HomeServices

Budge Huskey
CEO Coldwell Banker

Mark Willis
CEO Keller Williams Realty

Pam O'Connor
CEO Leading RE

Bob Hale
CEO Houston Assn of Realtors

Rob Hahn
Notorious R.O.B

Curt Beardsley
Realtor.com

Chris Crocker
Zillow

T3 Summit - Trends - Technology - Thought

Who should attend this event?

The **T3 Summit** is specifically targeted toward CEOs and other C-Level Thought Leaders who are shaping, will influence and/or wish to redefine the $55+ billion residential real estate brokerage business.

This is a strategic leadership summit which is not intended for real estate sales associates. The event is limited to only 250 Thought Leaders, which ensures a focused, intimate, high-impact experience for all. To maintain the integrity of 'thought,' there is no trade exhibition, and no back-of-room sales are permitted. Further, no 'selling from stage' is allowed. The event is all about thought, growth and meaningful relationship creation - not selling.

Predictions seem obvious with advance knowledge...

"This was by far the most actionable, inspiring meeting of the minds that I have ever been a part of. If you lead an organization, T3 is not optional; it is mandatory."

— **Glenn Sanford,** CEO / President, eXp Realty

"Congratulations on having pulled T3 off so successfully – a true testament to your influence in our industry!"

— **Spencer Rascoff,** CEO, Zillow

JW MARRIOTT.

JW Marriott Las Vegas Resort & Spa
221 N Rampart Blvd
Las Vegas, Nevada 89145
Room Block Reservations, Call (702) 869-7777

Special T3 Summit rates are available.

Register Today at **T3Summit.com/register**

MULTIPLE LISTING SERVICES

Wisdom will only prevail if it's the desire and the will of all parties involved.

Multiple Listing Services

Over the past two decades I have been watching the MLS, its customers, benefactors and the outside world charge closer to what we termed "The Perfect Storm" in our 2007 *Swanepoel TRENDS Report*. I've tracked the evolution of the system and the technology that has advanced it and sometimes drawn it to places in the short-term that may not have been in the best interest of its long-term goals. And we warned of the dangers involved if all parties failed to address the steadily compounding issues that were leading up to the storm and urged the leadership on both sides not to allow a parochial focus blind them from seeing the potential danger that lay ahead.

Back then it was evident that the objectives of the MLS industry and those of the brokerage industry had reached a wide chasm and today they have never been further apart. And therein lies one of the key issues facing the industry; the parties have ceased to be partners and have become participants. As a result, during a time of rapid and dramatic change in the economy, politics and the industry, the MLSs and their Realtor® partners have ceased to effectively communicate.

The MLS faces continual and growing policy challenges with respect to who can do what with the data and on what terms and conditions. Mix with that the revenue need that comes with keeping up with the technology challenge and it's no wonder that a communication gap has developed. But while MLSs have continued to debate the rules and policies concerning the data and whether or not they are to become public websites and promote listings, brokers and agents have swarmed to the Internet to promote their listings.

In the same way that third-party sites were able to capture the Internet in terms of consumer eyeballs on real estate while the industry had its head in the sand, a similar dynamic will occur as the participants to this issue compete rather than cooperate as partners. However, the threat to MLS isn't just from third-party providers but from within the industry.

From my perspective this is a huge opportunity for the Thought Leaders of the industry (especially those involved with the MLS) to sit down at the mediation table and work through the issues. There are valid concerns and issues on both sides of the table, but to allow those to fester serves no value to the user and consumer, merely those holding out, being stubborn or making threats. This issue can of course not be resolved in a few pages in a Report, and maybe the T3 Summit will be a great place to forward the discussion. Meanwhile we wanted to open up the thinking and asked different parties to provide some insight to the question:

QUESTION

Will the current trend toward "Off MLS Marketing" (pre-listings, pocket listings, private exclusive listings, etc.) continue to grow over the next three to five years or will it be a flash in the pan?

DALERoss
CEO - REALTOR® Property Resource

Off Market Listings or Pocket Listings have always been part of the marketing experience.

On occasions there may be specific reasons for waiting to market the property such as staging, a sellers request related to a family matter or other personal factors. However, today it's more a function of market conditions. Three years ago there were very few Off Market Listings since in most markets the inventory of properties completely overwhelmed the demand. In many markets there were 24-36 months of inventory supply. When a listing was taken the agent needed to expose the property to as many outlets as possible in hopes that there may be one potential buyer for that property.

accuracy, the desire for an agent or a company to retain both sides of the transaction may be more desirable.

> The desire for an agent or a company to retain both sides of the transaction may be more desirable.

Today the reverse is true. With a larger supply of purchasers and a lack of inventory (in most markets) many agents are experiencing multiple offers with some properties selling three to five percent over the listed price. Many of these properties are sold within hours or days of the listing and prior to being entered into the MLS. The fast pace of these market conditions sets the expectation that a listing may sell without MLS assistance. Even though, without the property listed in the MLS, it may diminish a CMA's

In order to avoid the continued increase in Off-Market Listings, market conditions must change. As market conditions become more balanced over the next 12-18 months with a more moderate flow of potential purchasers and a more even supply of properties in the market, the pace of properties selling quickly will change to a slower and more even pace. When this happens the need to once again insure that all listings are immediately placed in the MLS will be necessary to obtain a faster sale for owner.

ERROL Samuelson

Chief Strategy Officer - Move, Inc.

Pocket Listings, Whisper Listings, In-House Exclusives, Off-Market Listings—regardless of what they're called—that don't appear in MLSs and are marketed exclusively by an agent or among a select circle of agents have been around for years. There are circumstances where these listings make sense.

For example, a homeowner is undecided about selling and wants to test the market; a homeowner has privacy or security concerns; or a property may only appeal to a very niche audience.

However, during 2013 the number of pocket listings soared in some markets. For example, MLSListings, the MLS based in Silicon Valley, reported that "off-market listings" jumped from twelve percent of sales in 2011 to twenty-one percent in 2013, and were on pace to register more than $5 billion in sales for the year. Several factors have contributed to this increase but the most important

factor is market conditions. Nationally, inventory is at record lows. During the 2013 spring market, average active listings fell to 1.7 million, down fifteen percent year-on-year, and significantly below the high-water mark of 3.1 million in September 2007. Market time was also down nineteen percent year-on-year; 83 days. In some markets these conditions were more pronounced: San Francisco Bay Area, Sacramento, Seattle, Phoenix, Denver, Detroit, and Washington D.C. had significantly lower selling times. For example, this spring Contra Costa County in the Bay Area saw a 14 day median time-on-market.

A second factor is technology. Marketing listings among an elite circle of peers is becoming easer. Agents are forming "listing clubs" where they share listings on Facebook. In March, Chicago-based brokerage @properties released an app called @gent (developed by Yapmo), which enables its 1100 agents share information about properties before they hit the market (@properties is positioning the app as an agent-to-agent communications tool rather than a "pocket listings" platform, but agents nonetheless are

using it creatively). Redfin offers a service called Price Whisperer, where a homeowner can test the market by having a Redfin agent "pre-market" a property to up to 250 prospective buyers.

A third factor is a trend where some agents only wish to work with top producers in the belief that their transactions happen more efficiently, with better collaboration, and fewer opportunities for errors. As pocket listings have become more prevalent, so have concerns about the practice. NAR rules permit pocket listings with seller certification; however, sellers may not really understand the impact of keeping their listing off the MLS. Some brokers worry that agents are taking pocket listings without the brokers' knowledge or permission. This, in turn, is problematic due to the following risks:

- Fair Housing violations, if the property is only marketed to a select audience.

- Anti-trust issues, where only certain agents or brokers are chosen for cooperation.

- Compensation concerns, where buyers' agents are not assured payment without the MLS's guarantee of cooperation and compensation.

- Possible ethics violations: the NAR code of ethics states that Realtors® have a responsibility to protect and promote the best interests of their client (Article 1) and must cooperate with other real estate professionals (Article 3). Agents also have a responsibility to present all offers objectively and quickly

The largest concerns, however, relate to the home seller's ability to receive a fair price and the long-term impact on MLS. An MLSListings survey of 2000 agents found that 74 percent believed pocket listings reduced the likelihood that a home seller would receive the best price. Historically, the U.S. and Canada have been unique in their robust MLS infrastructure, which ensured broad marketing of listed properties and strong incentives for an army of buyers' agents to sell them.

When a significant number of properties are sold "off-MLS" the quality and predictive capability of the MLS, a shared common resource, is undermined. When sales are not entered into the MLS, or input with "zero days on market," price assessments and market trend information become unreliable. There is also a threat (albeit a low-probability threat) to the overall MLS ecosystem. Today, the MLS is the de-facto marketplace where sellers and buyers connect, via their agent representatives. In a post-MLS era, a listing agent could take a pocket listing, post that listing to the public real estate portals with their tens of millions of monthly users, and the portals would become the marketplace. In that scenario, the convening power and market regulating functions of the MLS would disappear and potentially not be recreated by other players.

The portals would also gain pricing power and potentially broader rights over the listing data. For example, realestate.com.au, the leading public portal in Australia, a country without robust MLS, had 2013 (FY) revenues of $190 million in the residential real estate sector. If similar per-capita revenues were generated in a post-MLS U.S., the top listing portal would generate $2.6 billion annually, an order of magnitude greater than current portal revenues, and an amount representing more than 50 percent of the estimated marketing spend by the residential real estate industry across all advertising channels.

A number of solutions have been proposed to address the challenges of pocket listings, including the concept of "Coming Soon" or pre-market listings, which appear in MLS for a limited period of time (seven to fourteen days) before being broadly marketed. Some have suggested a "sneak peek" feature on public portals to create hype for multiple offers and potentially freeze interested buyers until a property is ready to be listed.

As real estate markets return to equilibrium (as inventories rise to meet demand) and as price appreciation returns to more typical levels (both of which were observed in the second half of 2013), home buyers will find pocket listings less appealing. Also, agents who take pocket listings are becoming increasingly aware of their obligations to thoroughly educate home sellers on the associated benefits and risks. MLSs, however, will do well to seriously consider

> Marketing listings among an elite circle of peers is becoming easier.

the impact of social networks agent clubs, and the potential for these to disrupt their place in the real estate ecosystem. MLSs need to embrace and adopt the technology and marketing strategies being employed by pocket listers, because while the phenomenon has been accelerated by market conditions, these underlying technologies have the potential to disrupt the MLS community.

BRUCEZipf

President & CEO - NRT, Inc.

I do not believe that the recent rise in off-MLS marketing in certain markets by a relatively small percentage of brokers is the beginning of a national change in the industry.

I think this is just a blip driven by market imbalances. The market is correcting and we will see off-market activity begin to decline in the coming year.

Pocket listings have always been part of the business—primarily in conjunction with exotic properties, celebrity sellers or exclusive areas. The recent advent of pocket listings occurring beyond their traditional niche has been driven by the extremely short supply of homes in certain market areas. Buyer demand has been so strong and the inventory so limited that sellers have been able to achieve or beat their desired sales price without being on the MLS. However, the market is beginning to correct. This short supply of inventory has led to increased average sale prices and we see this driving an increase in the number of new homes being listed for sale. This balancing out of the market will bring seller and buyer demand back in line with more "normal" levels of activity where off-MLS marketing will not be successful in meeting seller price expectations.

Going beyond issues of supply and demand, I have a strong belief that properties should always be put on the MLS. We do have celebrity or very high-end sellers who wish to be discreet for privacy reasons and our agents of course will serve their clients as they desire. However, we make the case to these sellers that the benefits of being on the MLS will normally outweigh their concerns, and we make sure our sellers are fully informed of the pros and cons of this decision. Most of our sellers who start by staying off the MLS will often later decide to go on it, with positive results.

Furthermore, we take our fiduciary responsibility to our sellers very seriously. One of the most important services our sales associates provide is exposing properties

to the greatest pool of buyers in order to obtain the most attractive offer for a seller's property. This can only be accomplished by distributing the listing to as many sources as possible and that process begins by placing the property on the MLS. This distribution becomes even more critical when you factor in how buyers use the Internet and how the potential buyer pool has grown to be more national and even more global. The need to reach out to them and expose properties to a greater reach is more critical than ever in order to achieve the most successful sale. Pocket listings can't hope to match this optimal level of exposure.

In short, I believe that not only will market forces correct the recent increase in pocket listings in certain markets, our industry will be all the more healthy because of it. There will always continue to be unique sellers and situations where it makes sense to do a pocket listing, but this will and should always remain the rare exception and not the rule.

JIMHarrison

President and CEO - MLSListings

At the risk of sounding cliché, listings marketed outside of the MLS have been real estate's dirty little secret for decades.

Today's technology has made it easy to take the practice online, whereas before these properties were shared selectively in many formats, including unstructured broker networks. But I don't believe that the frequency of this practice is our true issue. Our issue is the increasing number of private listing companies, and the creation of virtual clubs by brokers and agents for whom the practice (whether large or small), that will remain hard-baked into their business model. These business models and practices reveal to us a future trend.

There are of course legitimate reasons why a property is kept off the MLS, such as getting it ready to sell or to protect the privacy of a seller who feels that way. Apparently, though, with today's low inventory numbers, a lot more sellers are concerned with their privacy than they were when inventory levels were higher.

As we conducted a deep dive to analyze the incidence of listings marketed off of the MLS in Northern California, we found more than numbers. We found pockets of practices in the form of either public or secret clubs that no amount of fines would discourage. If we pay attention to the trends, we can see that the number of listings marketed outside of the MLS environment increase during challenging market times and decline when inventory becomes available. In Silicon Valley the sales volume of off MLS transactions in our marketplace toppled $3 billion for 2012. One of our many indicators of these deals are a days on market reporting of zero. Double-ending in our market area is at 9.6 percent for the first half of this year while it was 9.2 percent for all of 2012. As we shared our methodology and information with MLSs around the U.S., many said that unbeknownst to them, secreting listings was a solid practice in their markets, also.

But again, I believe we can't stop at the numbers to identify a future trend, we have to look at the practice and what it tells us. It tells us that some brokers and agents want to feel they can control both ends of a transaction. We can also surmise that there are brokers and agents, unhappy with their MLS, who see private listings as a viable option. And I believe we will see multiple versions of broker-controlled listings and more private networks in the future. How secret they remain will be determined by their relationships with their MLS and the ability of both to find common ground of business support.

RUSSBergeron
Chief Executive Officer - Midwest Real Estate Data

First of all let me state that there is no such thing as a pocket listing. A pocket listing implies that one is not exposing that listing to anyone else. We all know that's false, because without some kind of exposure—be it limited to just your friends, a few other agents, a few other offices, or throughout the entire MLS membership—the property would never be sold. You either have an MLS listing or an off-MLS listing.

THE DETRIMENTS TO NOT USING THE MLS

The most significant detriment for not using the MLS is the minimal exposure a property receives when it's not placed in the MLS. MRED has over 35,000 real estate professionals constantly searching and viewing properties in our database. At any one time we have over 200,000 potential buyers entered into the system. Every listing is matched against those prospects to see if it matches the listing's price and characteristics. If the listing's price is changed, all of those prospects are searched again to see if it now matches more prospects. This is an ongoing process, with hundreds of potential buyers added into the system every day. No other system can match this pool of buyers.

By having a large pool of listings—our system currently has over 60,000 active residential properties—the seller and broker also have a better chance of identifying and choosing the best possible price for that listing so that it will be on the market for the least amount of time and will garner top dollar.

There are other potential threats to brokers should they decide to market a property outside the MLS and each of them could lead to an expensive legal challenge.

- Why is it being withheld? Is the broker putting his or her own interests ahead of the sellers?

- Could keeping a listing out of the MLS only to show to the "right buyers" be seen as a fair housing issue?

- Could limiting access to the listing to only a few select offices (who may be competitors) be viewed as an antitrust issue?

- Appraisers are skeptical of off-MLS listings because they haven't been properly vetted through MLS exposure. Does the price of an off-MLS sold property reflect a too-low price or a too-high price? The MLS better determines what the market price of a property should be.

- Could a seller feel cheated should they learn that a similar property received a higher sales price through the MLS than they did through an off-MLS listing? An August 19, 2013, article in the San Francisco Gate (Pocket Listings Grow as More Sellers Keep Homes Off the MLS) tells of a couple buying an off-MLS listing for $100,000 less than a similar house on the same street. Do you suppose the person who sold them the house might feel cheated?

INCENTIVE FOR AN AGENT TO NOT PUT A PROPERTY ON THE MLS

In a hot market, one reason might be the perceived value of avoiding having to pay another broker a cooperative commission and keeping it all in-house. In many cases this could mean the listing broker making more money on the transaction. Other arguments I've heard claim that by limiting exposure to just "top producers" ensures that via my peers I am assured of establishing the correct list price. I personally disagree with this theory since what better pool than the MLS to establish an acceptable price.

seriously challenged as soon as any marketing begins for the property.

MLS HELPS AN AGENT SELL A PROPERTY

The MLS has been around in some form for over a century. It's probably the most effective cooperative marketing tool found in any industry. Where else can you find competitors willing to cooperate and share compensation as we do within an MLS? The massive exposure that it gives a property throughout the market makes it the most effective advertising/marketing vehicle, period.

KEEPING OFF-MLS FROM BEING USED

Since we can't easily track the volume of off-MLS listings, it is difficult to say if they're increasing or no but they've definitely received a lot more attention recently. This may be due to the power of the Internet or the formation of private "listing clubs." I feel it's mostly due to the reduced inventory of listings that has made the use of off-MLS listings more noticeable to brokers who are desperately looking for properties to match up with their buyers.

MLSs have no interest in controlling the business model of any broker. Our job is to ensure that there is

> The most significant detriment for not using the MLS is the minimal exposure a property receives when it's not placed in the MLS.

The other age-old argument is celebrity sales. It has been my experience that this is a bogus argument because most celebrities use their status to help market their property so an off-MLS listing would make no sense. Why also do the top portals—Zillow, Trulia, realtor.com— all have celebrity real estate sections, which I have heard are the most popular areas on their sites?

The only valid arguments for off-MLS listings are the privacy and security concerns, but this argument is

compliance with our rules. We developed a recommended form that brokers may use to communicate to their sellers the consequences of choosing an off-MLS listing.

REPORTING OFF-MLS LISTINGS

We encourage our brokers to report to us if they are taking an off-MLS listing, but it's not required. We will ask for them to submit a seller's exemption should we get

DID YOU KNOW

75

PERCENT

of the contributors in this Report are ranked among the Top 200 Most Powerful People in Real Estate?

SWANEPOEL
POWER200
SP200.COM

a report of a property being offered for sale by one of our members that has not been entered into the system. We encourage our customers to report violations of any of our rules. An off-MLS listing in and of itself isn't a violation of our rules, as long as the appropriate exemption form is executed by the seller.

ENSURE DATA IS ACCURATE IF OFF-MLS LISTINGS ARE HAPPENING

Theoretically, MLS data could be affected by massive amounts of off-MLS listings. At this point in time, while we have seen an apparent increase in off-MLS listings during the peak of the recent market, we are confident that the vast majority of the marketplace data is still making it into the MLS. This is either because listings are: (1) eventually entered into the MLS after testing the off-MLS market; (2) entered after being sold (agents see the value of the information being in the system for comparable purposes); or (3) were kept off-MLS legitimately while "pre-marketing" or staging was being completed.

SYNDICATION SITES LIKE ZILLOW VS. THE MLS

The major difference is that a MLS is the professional tool set for all brokers that provides more than just listing data. We also offer CMAs, prospecting, reporting, statistics, analyses, trending, down payment assistance programs, and any number of deliverables that can be extracted from the MLS database. The public-facing sites, which owe their existence to real estate brokers and MLSs, are an advertising based model that thrives on driving people to their sites in order to maximize their advertising revenue while MLSs provide professional services to real estate professionals. The MLS is still the source of the most accurate and timely information because we are real time and no one can compete with that.

THE FUTURE FOR OFF-MLS LISTINGS

Technology today has a way of impacting everything. It's much easier to create data bases, data sharing, marketing, social marketing, or whatever the next big thing is going to be. So there may very well be more disruption in the organized marketplace that we have created over the past 100 years. At the end of the day, however, whatever the end game, those playing will realize the need for organization, rules compliance and enforcement, accuracy, and timeliness—the very definition of an MLS.

MATTCohen
CTO - Clareity Consulting

There are some past real estate practices that are now explicitly illegal.

In the past, some agents, lenders, construction companies, and insurance companies paid referral fees to unlicensed individuals and engaged in other practices that inflated the costs of real estate transactions, which is obviously bad for consumers. It was a practice that was explicitly forbidden with the passing of RESPA in 1974. Similarly, dual agency has been under scrutiny due to the challenge of providing full representation to two sides simultaneously. Disclosures have been created that highly discourage the practice, reframing it as "limited representation," and the practice is now illegal in three states, with more states likely to come. If a practice is bad for consumers, it's not likely to stay legal for long.

Will the current trend towards off-MLS Listings continue to grow over the next three to five years? Our answer is, "We hope the practice is discouraged before it tarnishes the trust consumers have in Realtors®." We've already seen those "in the know" enact rules requiring MLS listing. In August of 2013 Fannie Mae said that it wouldn't approve short sales unless the property had had an active MLS listing for at least five straight days including a weekend.

Most MLS rules allow the listing agent to delay a property's entry into the MLS by one to three days, but at some point it's the agent's responsibility to give the listing market exposure in order to obtain the maximum price for the listing. Some might ask, "Is MLS entry really needed to get top dollar for a listing?" Where it has been studied so far, the answer has been, "Yes!" In one study, for every $100,000 of home sold, not having an MLS listing cost the sellers up to $15,000.

If the practice of off-MLS listing continues, we may expect one or more of the following outcomes:

1. The NAR will step up and require MLS entry as a standard of practice.

2. Attorneys will smell blood and start a class action lawsuit against brokerages, leading to the practice's decline.

3. A law will be passed prohibiting the practice.

Off-MLS listings may grow more prevalent for a time, but any practice that is bad for consumers will have a limited shelf-life. The only question is whether this practice will worsen perceptions of the industry before the trend fades away due to market conditions or is stopped by legal means.

Off-MLS listings may grow more prevalent for a time, but any practice that is bad for consumers will have a limited shelf-life.

SUMMARY, Opinion and Take Away

One thing is very clear from the answers in this chapter: no executive we spoke to loves off-MLS listings. It seems the only ones that do are the thousands agents who are creating them and that they will continue no matter what the industry's leaders think.

Similar to the chapter on organized real estate, the discussion was far more prescription, advocacy, and attempts to persuade rather than description and prediction.

The best example comes from Russ Bergeron, CEO of MRED, whose MLS has already taken a firm stance against off-MLS listings. It's clear where he stands but what isn't as clear is whether he thinks they will grow over time or not. However, as he's concluding his polemic against off-MLS listings, he does say the following:

Technology today has a way of impacting everything. It's much easier to create databases, data sharing, marketing, social marketing, or whatever the next big thing is going to be. So there may very well be more disruption in the organized marketplace that we have created over the past 100 years. At the end of the day, however, whatever the end game, those playing will realize the need for organization, rules compliance and enforcement, accuracy, and timeliness—the very definition of an MLS.

Keep that definition and the need in mind for a moment. Because Bergeron's peer, Jim Harrison, the CEO of MLSListings in Silicon Valley, serves in possibly one of the most heavily impacted markets with these pocket listing clubs, here's what he has to say:

We found pockets of practices in the form of either public or secret clubs that no amount of fines would discourage.

And also:

We can also surmise that there are brokers and agents, unhappy with their MLS, who see private listings as a viable option. And I believe we will see multiple versions of broker-controlled listings and more private networks in the future.

What is so interesting about this chapter is that these off-MLS listings have been a feature of the industry for years. Every single commentator noted that, usually with the hopeful and slightly dismissive wave of the hand: "Don't worry, once this crazy seller's market corrects back to normal this whole thing will be a nonfactor."

Bruce Zipf, the CEO of NRT, the largest brokerage in the U.S. by quite a lot noted that:

This short supply of inventory has led to increased average sale prices and we see this driving an increase in the number of new homes being listed for sale. This balancing out of the market will bring seller and buyer demand back in line with more "normal" levels of activity where off-MLS marketing will not be successful in meeting seller price expectations.

And Dale Ross, CEO of RPR:

As market conditions become more balanced over the next 12-18 months with a more moderate flow of potential purchasers and a more even supply of properties in the market, the pace of properties selling quickly will change to a slower and more even pace. When this happens the need to once again insure that all listings are immediately placed in the MLS will be necessary to obtain a faster sale for owner.

However, the technologists who responded do note that yes, off-MLS listings have been around for a while, and yes, off-MLS activity is a function of market fundamentals, but… there is something going on here.

Errol Samuelson, the CEO of Realtor.com:

A second factor is technology. Marketing listings among an elite circle of peers is becoming easier. Agents are forming listing clubs where they share listings on Facebook. In March, a Chicago-based brokerage, @properties released an app called @gent (developed by Yapmo), which enables its 1,100 agents share information about properties before they hit the market (@properties is positioning the app as an agent-to-agent communications tool rather than a pocket listings platform, but agents nonetheless are using it creatively). Redfin offers a service called Price Whisperer, where a homeowner can test the market by having a Redfin agent "pre-market" a property to up to 250 prospective buyers.

Samuelson further recommends:

MLSs, however, will do well to seriously consider the impact

of social networks agent clubs, and the potential for these to disrupt their place in the real estate ecosystem. MLSs need to embrace and adopt the technology and marketing strategies being employed by pocket listers, because while the phenomenon has been accelerated by market conditions, these underlying technologies have the potential to disrupt the MLS community.

If brokers think off-MLS listings are just a fad, and Samuelson takes the phenomenon seriously, Matt Cohen of Clareity wants to declare war on them. He wants someone to put a stop to the practice, if changes to market conditions don't wipe it out first:

If the practice of off-MLS listing continues, we may expect one or more of the following outcomes:

- *The NAR will step up and require MLS entry as a standard of practice.*
- *Attorneys will smell blood and start a class action lawsuit against brokerages, leading to the practice's decline.*

- *A law will be passed prohibiting the practice.*

Off-MLS listings may grow more prevalent for a time, but any practice that is bad for consumers will have a limited shelf-life. The only question is whether this practice will worsen perceptions of the industry before the trend fades away due to market conditions or is stopped by legal means.

While we are in general agreement with most of the commentators that off-MLS listings activity will likely fade into obscurity if the market conditions change, there are a few trends here worth looking at further, especially over the next three to five years. The issue of off-MLS listings taken in isolation in and of itself is not a big thing, just as Bruce Zipf says.

But we take a broader view from high atop the theoretical mountain to spot trends before they become obvious. Consider the discussions in Chapter 4 about the future of organized real estate. It was patently obvious from that chapter that dissatisfaction with ORE is at an all time high. Consider further the discussion from Chapter 3 and 5 about the future of brokerage models and the value of brokerage brands as we weave this tapestry together.

BROKER INCENTIVES

Broker dissatisfaction with the MLS structure is extremely high right now. As Samuelson points out, the private listing has been around forever; the only thing that has changed over time is that technology has made the ability to share listings privately far easier. As he noted, a Chicago brokerage, @Properties, has created a mobile app to enable the easy sharing of information (and a listing is just that—information) for its agents previous to entry into the MLS. Facebook Groups require zero programming, but agents can use them to create secret listing clubs amongst themselves.

Why would @Properties create such an app? As we saw from discussions about brokerage models, brokerages are under significant pressure today as the personality-driven relationship-based business that was brokerage has given way to a show-me-the-money-now and what-have-you-done-for-me-lately business that is brokerage

> Broker dissatisfaction with the MLS structure is extremely high right now.

today. Real estate agents are far too untethered from the brokerage, and broker value is up in the air.

The incentive for brokerages to create tools like @ Properties has is overwhelming today. @Properties did not invest in @gent to waste money or to break rules or to cheat sellers; they did it to increase the value of @Properties to their agents.

TECHNOLOGY IS EASY

One of the main takeaways from the off-MLS listing issue is that if technology was once a barrier to entry to offer MLS services, it no longer is. Bergeron's definition now takes on a slightly different meaning:

At the end of the day, however, whatever the end game, those playing will realize the need for organization, rules compliance and enforcement, accuracy, and timeliness—the very definition of an MLS.

What word doesn't appear on that list? Technology. Because Bergeron knows that the actual technology of the MLS is now widely available. In some respects, one could run a MLS out of a secret Facebook Group, as long as "organization, rules compliance and enforcement, accuracy, and timeliness" were also provided. Which we think is slightly asymmetric to the way most people view this issue.

GROWTH AND TRANSFORMATION

Broker-created or broker-sanctioned off-MLS activity is nothing more than the office meeting taken online. We don't think lawyers will bother, unless there is real lack of notice to and consent by the seller. We certainly cannot imagine government passing laws against off-MLS activity (at least, not without at the same time making the MLS into a public utility, which is a whole different issue). And given the dissatisfaction with the NAR, with the attendant predictions of a much smaller country club style NAR, we can't easily imagine it passing some Code of Ethics violation that would make a difference.

What's more, this sort of broker-sanctioned sharing is not market dependent. Brokerages have been holding office meetings in seller's markets and in buyer's markets and there is no reason to think broker-powered off-MLS tools would be any different.

The agent-driven pocket-listing clubs may fade away, especially if the market changes significantly, but the wide availability of technology is likely to legitimize the practice and allow it to be implement in different formats. Over the next few years we believe that off-MLS activity is actually expected to gain some momentum. They may not be called "pocket listings " but in effect, that is precisely what they will be.

DID YOU KNOW?

38 PERCENT of the attendees of 2013's T3 Summit are Chairmans, CEOs, Presidents, and Founders

38%	**Chairman	CEO	President**
18%	**Vice President** (Operations, Marketing, Strategy Technology, Sales, Alliances, etc.)
17%	**Broker	Owner**
14%	**Manager	Director** (Innovation, Sales, Relocation, Product Management, Engagement)
8%	**Other C-Level Executives** (COO, CTO, Chief Strategy Officer, CMO, Chief Thinking Officer)
5%	**Associate Broker	Sales Associate**

SWANEPOEL
T3SUMMIT
LAS VEGAS | 2014

APRIL 9 - 11, 2014

THE MOBILITY OF CONNECTIVITY

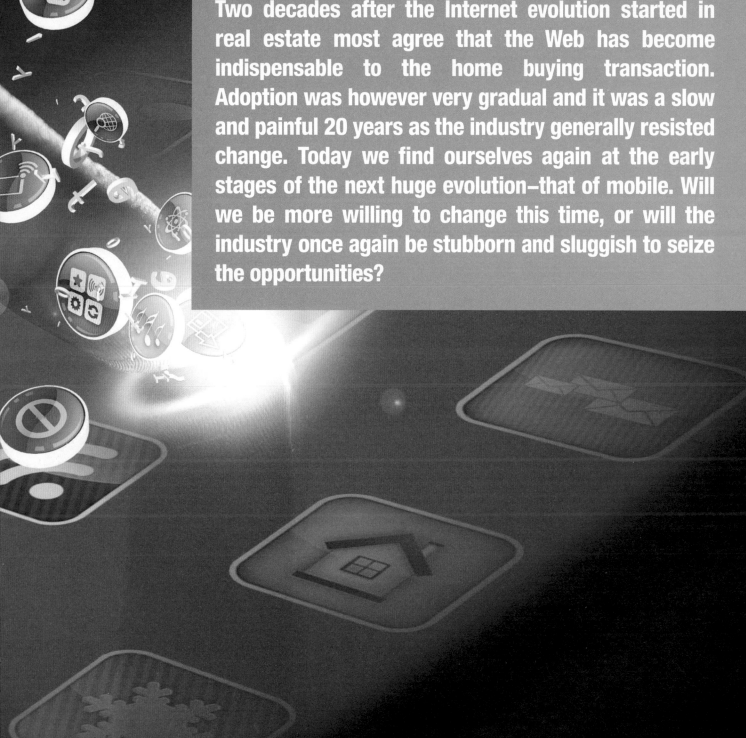

Two decades after the Internet evolution started in real estate most agree that the Web has become indispensable to the home buying transaction. Adoption was however very gradual and it was a slow and painful 20 years as the industry generally resisted change. Today we find ourselves again at the early stages of the next huge evolution–that of mobile. Will we be more willing to change this time, or will the industry once again be stubborn and sluggish to seize the opportunities?

The Mobility of Connectivity

What may seem logical and should be implemented immediately sometimes takes years, even decades, before it becomes commonplace. So, yes, the Internet and mobile are mainstream, but it's been a two-decade journey. Both these innovations are however so huge that they each carry within themselves a large number of sub structures and trends. So, what's next?

In this chapter we explore the impact of the Internet and mobile as game changers to our beloved industry. Yes, everyone has a Smartphone and most have another wireless device like a tablet. Sure we use them daily for all the regular tasks like calls, messaging, information gathering and networking. But are we ready to use them for more? Can we as an industry take a fundamental business shift and maximize the enormous potential these business-changing tools are offering or does it take an outsider to show us?

The portals have shown us that the consumer has (and continues) to love stimulating and enchanting ways of accessing information. And mobile and apps make accessing the web easier and more fun. Aggregator websites report that in the week 60 percent of their traffic is via mobile devices and on the weekends that number jumps to 70 percent. Zillow even reported for the third quarter of 2013 that they had 120 homes being viewed every second via mobile. So we reached out to some Thought Leaders with this question:

QUESTION

In a different way than what we experience today, how will the Internet and mobile technology in the next three to five years further enhance and/or redefine (read impact) the value proposition of the agents' contribution to the home buying/selling transaction?

MARKWillis

CEO - Keller Williams Realty International

I think it's been a commonly held belief in recent years that we've been on a path where technology would overtake the industry and make agents obsolete, but I think we can now say with confidence that will not be the case.

Instead, a perfect storm has erupted, where consumers, who expect to have technology available to them while purchasing real estate, have met with real estate companies that are finding new ways to make their businesses run more fluidly. That's why I think companies that implement a business model that is agent-centric and technology-driven will experience the most growth in terms of market share and revenue over the next five years.

We've observed that some of the major tech-based companies in the industry are failing to capture significant

market share and sustain profit because of one major flaw; they're using agents to support their technology instead of using technology to support their agents. A common misconception about technology is that it has (or will) "change the business." In our experience, it hasn't changed the business, just the way we do business. The means through which we reach our customers—from land lines to mobile phones to email and text—has evolved radically thanks to technology; however, the conversation hasn't fundamentally changed.

Companies that use agents to support their technology are facing a variety of issues with the types of leads they attract, in part because they've made internet lead generation their bread-and-butter, which, unfortunately for them, is a tool that primarily produces buyer leads. Without a considerable amount of listings, these companies are left with minimal room for market share growth. However, I think if they were to step away from that model and become more agent-centric, they would not be chained to buyer heavy lead generation tactics, and could support agents in developing ways to target and convert listing leads.

There are plenty of advantages for companies that use an online platform, one important one being that they've used the Internet to provide transparency through the use of public consumer ratings. Just like if I want to go to a great restaurant, I'm going to go look one up on Yelp, when I want to find a good real estate agent, I'm going to search for what others are saying about them online. Some tech-based, agent-centric companies have done a great job of publicizing their agents' consumer ratings, understanding that the number one reason home buyers and sellers choose their agent is their reputation.

It's important that agent-centric companies incorporate technology into their business models, because it's where most people begin their real estate journey. Whether it's through a Smartphone app that can show them the price of any home near their current location, or just casually browsing for homes online, consumers are increasing their appetite for technology driven companies—giving businesses a choice to either feed that appetite or risk not growing.

SHERRYChris

President & CEO - Better Homes and Gardens Real Estate

Over the last several years, there has been a lot of talk about "mobile strategies." No one could argue the importance of having a manifestation of your brand or business in a "mobile environment" for the "mobile consumer."

It was the flame that ignited the mobile arms race. Everyone built an app and many built a mobile website. Agents began conducting larger portions of their business via their mobile devices—phones and tablets alike.

During the next three to five years that will go away. Shocked? Don't worry... I'm not saying mobile's importance will go away—quite the opposite. It will become so big, so prevalent, so core that agents (and brokers and brands) will no longer say "I have a mobile strategy." It will simply be the strategy. Agents will become mobile-non mobile amphibians, not even noticing that

> We live in exponential times. The pace of change is break-neck.

they conduct X percent of their business on their tablet or phone and Y percent of their business on their computer. They will just conduct business— seamlessly across all channels. Likewise, the 24 by 7 service imperative to the consumer will become second nature.

No one will say "I need to be available at all times and in all ways to my consumer." They just will or they will be left behind. Today, industry thought leaders throw around statistics such as "X percent of people begin the real estate transaction on their mobile device" or "Y percent of agents have a smart phone." We throw out those stats to try to spring the late adopters into action. Those statistics won't even be relevant in the next three to five years. The time for that justification will have passed. We will just do it.

We live in exponential times. The pace of change is break-neck. The cost of not acting on something today—a trend, a new technology, a new way of thinking—is incalculable. There is no way to catch up. The industry will be divided into those who did, and those who didn't. Those who lived to fight another day, to win another customer and those who didn't.

HELEN HANNACasey

President - Hanna Holdings

According to Business Insider, some experts have predicted that mobile will overtake desktop users by 2014 and become the consumers' norm for accessing the Internet; a complete personalized experience for each online user.

As brokers work to engage more consumers and secure genuine leads for their agents, they will need to tie a value proposition into their digital offerings.

A solid digital offering is no longer a gimmick when going on a listing presentation; it's a key component to secure the listing. Tools like Google Glass will allow agents to give prospective home buyers an actual personalized virtual tour while the buyer walks down the street.

However, technology won't replace the value of agents or what they offer; instead it will be used to help accelerate the home buying process. We don't believe that any technology will replace smart, articulate, and educated agents, but at the same time they can no longer wait for the customer to search and then show them the homes they have selected. Brokers must engage the consumer and the agent at the same time.

> We don't believe that any technology will replace smart, articulate, and educated agents.

As an industry, we must respond to our future buyers' and sellers' needs by giving them the additional knowledge that they can't find on other sites. We believe that, contrary to the opinion that some agents are behind in technology, we have always been on the cutting edge and mobile is our future. The value proposition comes from brokers who create new mobile technology to make the home buying process simpler and easier for the consumer. Personalization, convenience, and speed, in my opinion, will be the driving forces of technology in the near future.

I have to run since my Galaxy Smartphone watch is ringing and I have to respond to messages on my Google Glass. Seriously, we are testing both. I applied for the Google Glass Explorer and I am experimenting to see if there is value for our company and agents. The watch phone is just for fun.

IAN Morris

CEO - Market Leader (A subsidiary of Trulia)

The shift from the desktop to mobile is the most important technology trend we will see in the next three to five years. While this shift is already underway, it's nothing compared to what's ahead.

On the surface, this change may not seem monumental to the lives of real estate professionals, but like the earlier move from off line to the web, the downstream implications of this shift to mobile are far reaching. The change won't revolutionize the transaction, nor will it negatively impact the critical role that seasoned real estate professionals play in it. But, consumer migration to the mobile web will strongly favor the franchisors, brokerage companies, and agents that are best equipped to take advantage of this opportunity to increase their market share. There are two reasons for this.

MOBILE IS DRIVING TRAFFIC TO NATIONAL SITES.

Rapid consumer adoption of home search via mobile is a trend that is driving a greater percentage of searchers to well-known national sites. This trend began years ago due to the significant technology investments and expertise that were required to support innovative web-based home search sites. However, those investments were minor compared to what is now required to continuously innovate not only on the web, but also across many different mobile apps and platforms. As a result, more and more consumer leads will flow from the best known sites.

But as we know, lead generation is only a piece of the puzzle. Success at the local level is driven first and foremost by the tools and expertise that brokerage companies and their agents use to cultivate those leads and turn prospects into clients.

MOBILE IS DRIVING CONSOLIDATION OF REAL ESTATE TOOLS

The cost of creating and maintaining innovative tools for real estate professionals across both web and now mobile platforms is growing rapidly. As a result, most of the small, local software vendors that many firms have looked to in the past will no longer have the financial resources or technical expertise needed to stay in the game.

As such, forward looking brokerage companies who have chosen to provide tools for their agents, but who have looked to small firms for key components, are now looking upstream to larger players with the resources and expertise to provide multi-platform innovation in the years to come.

While the impact of mobile on the consumer experience is already evident in our space, much of the impact it will have on professionals is yet to come. This is very good news for visionary firms and practitioners who will use this sea change to increase their market share by building their presence where consumers are now searching, and using the right tools to help convert more of these prospects into happy clients.

TOMFerry
Founder & CEO - Your Coach

Many traditional agent activities can now be done remotely, from home search and market research to document signing.

These new tools allow for quicker response time or "speed to lead," resulting in more appointments, greater accessibility to home and neighborhood knowledge, and increased transactions. The paperless, mobile agent is still not the mainstream. As an early adopter, they can do almost anything transaction-related on a mobile device. These savvy agents can close a fair number of transactions without paying for additional staff and still have a life. This is a huge difference from the past and a game changer for profitability. The consumer of the future will only know a tech savvy agent.

IS IT OK IF THE HOMEBUYER DOES SOME OF TASKS PREVIOUS DONE BY AGENTS?

It has to be. Homebuyers have the ability to research everything, from real estate agents and home permits to the home inspector and lender reviews. While homebuyers are becoming more aware the information still must be verified, resulting in a continuous need for knowledgeable listing agents, buyer representatives, and agents that show homes.

HOW CAN AN AGENT STILL REMAIN IMPORTANT TO HOMEBUYERS AND SELLERS?

Agents can remain important by taking on the role of trusted advisor. Sharing real market data and analysis, being informed locally and globally, and embracing the emotional experience of homebuyers and sellers is

something only a real estate agent can do. Every agent should have the knowledge of housing trends that spans years in each of their communities they serve and the skills to communicate their value effectively. They need to have an expertise in negotiations to close the sale, and most importantly, the marketing savvy to attract a high quality number of buyers and sellers to serve, both on and off line.

DOES THIS SHIFT OF ACTIVITIES FREE AGENTS UP TO DO OTHER TASKS/ACTIVITIES? LIKE WHAT?

I don't believe it's freeing any time up. In fact, it may be making it more time intensive in a different way. Agents are shifting their activities, yet the primary focus for each agent still needs to be marketing to find new listings and buyers for those properties. Whereas once they may have spent hours on the property search process, with technology advances agents now find themselves as more of a resource, attempting to field and decipher data and client questions.

ARE AGENTS' PREPARED/EDUCATED FOR THIS NEW ROLE? WHAT SHOULD THEY DO SPECIFICALLY TO PREPARE?

Many agents aren't prepared, and those that are stand out as top producers. The use of technology and attending to the needs of online buyers requires structure and systems to be in place. To be most effective, every agent, whether running a team or acting alone, must understand their process and translate why and what they do for their clients. Agents need to take a closer look at their online buyer and recognize the need to nurture and understand each lead and then create an experience that can be replicated.

IN FIVE YEARS WHAT SHOULD A TOP PRODUCING AGENT BE DOING TO DELIVER A BETTER EXPERIENCE?

Top producing agents can deliver better experiences by streamlining processes and embracing technology. The best agents deliver top customer service and connect with their clients through speed and technology, simplicity and care, and delivering expected and outlined results. Agents who truly know their market and share local buying and selling information with their clients will continue to be top producers.

MATTHEW Beall

Co-Founder - Hawaii Life Real Estate Brokers

Transaction-related processes — loan applications, appraisals, title, escrow, and transaction management — are complex and bureaucratic and are major pain points for the real estate industry.

They're innumerable stupidities that require immense focus, time, and resources from buyers, sellers, brokers, agents, and anyone else involved.

These processes can and will be radically simplified with online and mobile software. Home buyers and sellers, as well as brokers and agents, expect the simplicity and efficiency that the Internet and mobile technology provide. They also expect all of the processes to be included in familiar interfaces.

As a result, the role of agents will have more to do with generating sales (listing, prospecting, negotiating, etc.), and they'll be able to oversee more transactions simultaneously, further increasing their influence.

The quality of real estate related data continues to improve. Public record data, historical sales information, current listings, website analytics, etc., are all consolidated and utilized, whether by large, publicly-traded companies, or by brokerages and agents. As a result the behavior of home buyers and sellers (in some cases, agents) is becoming more and more predictable.

Predicting behavior based on data is one thing but acting on those predictions is quite another. For agents, acting on the data means networking, matching buyers and sellers, and using data to (more) accurately advise buyers and sellers on pricing decisions.

The role of the agent includes continual quality control, such as adjusting data-driven market analyses for the real world, as well as applying trending information to the actual marketplace. For example: How many times does the average homebuyer view a listing online before requesting a showing? What's the average amount of time someone owns his or her home in a certain neighborhood?

As the quality of data increases, the agents' value will increase.

As the quality of the data increases, the agents' value will increase because they're the most likely candidates to act on, interpret, and scale the value of the information. The ability to interpret and act on data on behalf of a home buyer or seller, as well as the delivery and use of software that radically simplifies the "transaction-related processes," will radically increase the value of the agent in the next three to five years.

AUSTIN Allison
Co-Founder & CEO - dotloop

During the last 10 years we've made almost everything in the consumer world digital and accessible via mobile, with technologies such as email, mobile phones, and the Internet nearly eliminating face-to-face interaction. These shifts have changed nearly every industry (real estate included) and redefined the modern agent's role in its wake.

It's no longer the volumes of paperwork alone that plague the real estate industry. Digital and mobile technologies challenge agents to think differently about the value they provide to clients. With listings available to anyone with an Internet connection, agents' most important job is providing great experiences that clients love. During the next three to five years, and well beyond, agents must focus on fundamentally rethinking how they work to put people first and to create more personal, human experiences.

ELIMINATING WORK—DIGITIZATION

Innovation doesn't happen in digitizing existing processes and stringing together multiple applications, but in necessarily changing the way everyone in real estate works. Agents must reinvent how they work — not only to make the real estate process more enjoyable for clients (and consistent with our connected world) — but also make the lives of agents easier and more efficient. That means moving away from yesterday's technology that solved yesterday's problems. By eliminating the "work" that comes in the form of PDFs, siloed systems, and unnecessary back-and-forth between parties, we'll move this industry forward. This isn't a broker, association or agent decision. It's a consumer-driven decision, and agents must get on board in order to stay relevant.

ADAPTING TO THE NEW NORM
— CUSTOMER EXPERIENCE IS KING

It's no secret that this great industry has always been about people working together. The digital age simply

made the work possible at scale, but it pushed people to the periphery. To succeed, real estate leaders must put people and their emotions first again and think about their organizations as the sum of interactions between people. From encouraging e-signatures and offers on an iPhone and booking home inspection appointments with a click of a button, to using Social Media to increase inbound leads, the most successful brokers and agents are turning to new technologies to offer a more compelling, "people-centric" interaction. There's no going back.

Buyers and sellers are beginning to expect—and demand—that human experience when they make decisions. Agents who put people at the center of the equation, and create an enjoyable experience that's on their terms, are the ones who win big, retain customers, and receive referrals. Technology doesn't replace the agent, but rather, when applied wisely, it allows agents to focus on their top priority—clients. It's managing the entire transaction seamlessly from their iPhone instead of madly searching for a fax machine in the wee hours of the night. It's remembering to ask how their son's baseball tournament turned out. It's being the first to show them a house that just came on the market. Most importantly, it's about treating customers like people and not leads.

BERNICERoss
CEO - RealEstateCoach.com

The best strategy for real estate success today is micro-specialization coupled with early adoption of the latest Internet, mobile, and video trends.

While today's consumers normally visit the "big three" (Realtor.com, Trulia, and Zillow) as part of their search process, what they really crave is a wealth of information about the local lifestyle that these sites cannot provide. To illustrate this point, there is no app or technology that can tell a buyer whether this hillside property is dark six months a year, that the local owls sometimes hunt small pets, or that the view adds an additional $100,000 of value to this floor plan.

FROM BIG SCREEN TO SMALL SCREEN TO NO SCREEN

The next big opportunity for early adopters will be based upon changes in the devices consumers use to view listings. Your next iPhone could be an "eyephone"—literally a contact lens that allows you to receive text messages, email, and Social Media updates. Small screen design requires minimal written content specifically targeted to what viewers want most: what's for sale, what's my house worth, and neighborhood information.

On the other hand, fiber optics and broadband expansion are making digital big screen videos commonplace. HDTV quality property "movies" are already becoming an expectation in the luxury market. Nevertheless, large file sizes and slow download times may continue to hamper adoption on the small screen.

In the next few years, augmented reality apps will ultimately lead to "no screen." Augmented reality viewers allow buyers to see the view from their 23rd floor condo before the developer even breaks ground. International clients can view local signs, information on local landmarks, and a wealth of other hyperlocal information in their own language. Apps such as Iscape and Obeo's V-Stager already allow buyers to virtually landscape or decorate their future

homes as part of their search process. Instead of signing your offers on your mobile device, you will literally sign them in the air as you view the contracts through an augmented reality viewer. Geo-location coupled with other mobile authentication services will make your digital signatures more secure than ever before.

Tomorrow's most successful real estate agents will be hyperlocal lifestyle specialists, early adopters of the best new technologies, and most importantly, totally focused on providing their clients with the best possible purchasing or selling experience.

SUMMARY, Opinion and Take Away

The Internet entered the residential real estate brokerage, when in 1995 at a NAR convention, it was stated from the stage "Click a mouse and buy a house." Since then, entire industries have vanished while others were created and real estate has had a stormy and fulfilled romance with technology. While initially slow to adopt most technology strategies, we do, as an industry, once we decided to embrace a certain product, service or strategy, move forward with vengeance.

Technologist Ian Morris, formerly of MarketLeader and now of Trulia, says the shift from the desktop to mobile is now the next most important technology trend we will see in the next three to five years. While this shift is already underway, it's nothing compared to what's ahead. We agree with Morris.

Yes, brokers and agents all have a phone—a Smartphone and probably a tablet too— but we have generally not maximized the power of mobility and the power of connectivity the way we could and should. That has again let the door open for someone else to jump in. But the difference this time is that we already had large, well-funded companies in the real estate space—namely Zillow and Trulia—that were able to move quickly and seize a beachhead. Subsequently they have expanded the beachhead and basically taken over the space.

Today, in the mobile arena, Zillow, Trulia, and Realtor.com are so far ahead of the existing players that a reasonable observer would conclude that competition is strictly an affair between them, and that from a brokerage point of view it's already game over.

But maybe it's a race, for eyeballs and traffic, and it really doesn't impact the actual Realtor® that much.

Dynamo CEO of rapid growing Keller Williams Realty, Mark Wills, says this:

A common misconception about technology is that it has (or will) "change the business." In our experience, it hasn't changed the business, just the way we do business. The means through which we reach our customers—from landlines to mobile phones to email and text—has evolved radically thanks to technology; however, the conversation hasn't fundamentally changed.

Most of the commentary we received tracks Mark's thinking: the value of the agent hasn't changed, only the way agents talk to clients has. Gary Keller, the godfather of the agent team, spoke about innovation coming not from technologists but from agents. And we suspect that Mark Willis would agree, as he also strongly believes that agent-centric companies will find success while technology-centric companies will struggle.

However, Hawaii Life founder Matthew Beall gives us a specific vision of how he thinks the value of the agent will change:

The role of the agent includes continual quality control, such as adjusting data-driven market analyses for the real world, as well as applying trending information to the actual marketplace. For example: How many times does the average homebuyer view a listing online before requesting a showing? What's the average amount of time someone owns his or her home in a certain neighborhood?

As the quality of the data increases, the agents' value will increase because they're the most likely candidates to act on, interpret, and scale the value of the information. The ability to interpret and act on data on behalf of a home buyer or seller, as well as the delivery and use of software that radically simplifies the "transaction-related processes," will radically increase the value of the agent in the next three to five years.

What is left unanswered, except via circumstantial implication, is just how many agents even collect such data, never mind possess the ability to interpret and act on that data. Which is why Beal thinks that agents will be able to oversee more transactions simultaneously, further increasing their influence.

To the extent that thoughts on specific changes

are available, we think the trend is toward increased commoditization of the real estate agent, which has one near-term impact (already being seen) and one medium-term impact (not yet seen).

We know that during the last few years the impact of technology has been widely disparate. Some top agents are topping one record-setting year with another by leveraging the efficiency of technology. Others, however, are still desperately searching for some silver bullet solution.

So when Beall says agents will be able to oversee more transactions simultaneously, this does not mean everyone will complete more sales. Agents don't create more transactions—the number of sales is not affected by what agents do. So if agents are able to do more, then more agents will also need to do less, so as to balance the number out. We already have so many agents doing little or nothing that when technology amplifies this situation we really will have a bunch of zero-valued licensees. (As an industry this really needs to be addressed, but we will leave that debate for another Trends Report).

As the mundane tasks of the transaction itself—the paperwork, the signatures, the filling out of forms—become more and more automated and/or off-shored, these top producers can devote more and more time to business

processes in place to service the consumer adequately, nor can they market themselves effectively at scale. I couldn't agree more.

What makes this trend interesting is when we overlay some of the insights from the chapters on innovation, on organized real estate, and on brokerage business models onto the sentiments about technology and agent value. For example, consider this passage from Bob Bemis:

Professional practitioners must concentrate more on those portions of the process that require professional input and trained guidance and experience. The industry will no longer have a place for mere mechanics who can fill out forms, chauffeur buyers, and unlock lockboxes, but who offer little in the way of guidance or experience in those areas of the transaction where such guidance and experience is essential.

New entities will emerge to address other underserved segments of the real estate transaction process. This movement will further reduce the menu of services that mechanic agents can offer that the consumer can't acquire on their own. The real estate process is still highly fragmented. Separate services for home inspection, title insurance, closing services, pest certification, appraisal, document management,

> We know that during the last few years the impact of technology has been widely disparate. Some top agents are topping one record-setting year with another by leveraging the efficiency of technology. Others, however, are still desperately searching for some silver bullet solution.

development and customer service, leading to a virtuous cycle of more referral business. We think that the trend toward commoditization of the transaction process leads to the top producers taking more and more market share, at the expense of the middle class producers. These changes do not affect the part-timer doing real estate as a hobby or already doing zero.

A co-*New York Times* author and friend of mine, Tom Ferry, the noted coach and speaker, is forthright about it when he says that most agents are simply unprepared for the shift. Most do not have the structures and systems and

electronic signatures, escrow services, even potentially open house management, and concierge showing services are all areas that could see new web-based replacement offerings in the years to come. More momentous will be the combination and aggregation of such services into more complete web-based management systems used equally and cooperatively by agents and consumers alike.

Or this from Curt Beardsley:

The key initial questions that potential home sellers and

buyers currently ask of agents—how much is my home worth? Or what more can you tell me about this home?—will largely be answered without personal interaction. Home valuations (AVMs) will continue to improve with access to larger and more complete neighborhood and property profiles and will more completely take into consideration school and neighborhood desirability from consumer ratings and student scores: Home amenity improvements from local contractor and remodeler systems (the computer will actually have "seen" inside the home and know if there is granite countertops in

to deliver more and more insight direct to the consumer.

Now overlay onto these visions the continued disconnect of the agent from the physical bricks and mortars office and from the brokerage. If, as McClure wrote, using Google Hangout to attend an office meeting is adequate for agents, what makes it inadequate for buyers? "This is a relationship business" is no panacea, since there was a time when brokers and agents were also in relationship businesses. Google Helpout—the paid professional version of Hangout—is allowing an IT administrator in Romania to

> Both of these opinions are disruptive visions that go to the heart of the specifics of agent value to the transaction.

the kitchen); and the intangibles like "curb appeal" and desirableness based on online consumer behaviors. This will drive the I need to contact an agent action even closer to the transaction—meaning the consumer will be more engaged and connected to the online brands they use during their pre-contact searching—and will give these online brands significant influence in who the consumer eventually engages with… if they do.

Both of these opinions are disruptive visions that go to the heart of the specifics of agent value to the transaction.

Bemis' vision is essentially that anything that can be outsourced will be, from dealing with title to document management to driving buyers around and opening doors. The value of the agent will depend on "professional input, trained guidance, and experience."

Beardsley's vision takes that a step further. If AVM's become truly accurate, then the comparable analysis that Matt Beall describes as the core information-processing task of the agent goes away. After all, Realtors® are not infallible when they price a house. If intangibles like "curb appeal" can be quantified and algorithms can take over with predictive analytics, then the value of the agent decreases even further. Put differently, the areas of professional input, trained guidance, and experience shrink as the combination of big data and predictive analytics start

offer live video help to consumers in the U.S. Why not real estate advice, or pricing, or assistance with negotiating the deal?

We don't think we'll see this kind of virtual real estate via the "Philippines" any time soon. But what I want to show is that the elements are already all there and that some successful agents are using virtual transaction coordinators based overseas to perform many of the mechanical tasks of a home buying transaction. It's now only a short step from here to fully virtual real estate.

As I stated elsewhere in this Report, predicting the trend is easier than predicting the timeline, as the timeline is not ability-driven but emotionally driven. When will the real homebuyers be ready for a total, or near total virtual transaction? When will the real estate brokerage industry be ready? Could easily be another decade.

However, what we can state with more certainty is that in the near-term, the power of technology will continue to eliminate the middle class real estate agent and create more real estate superstars!

PORTALS

One of the most significant shifts occurring in the real estate industry over the past couple of years has been the rapid and remarkable growth in the power of the portals such as Zillow and Trulia.

Portals

Granted, the average online lead has nowhere near the same level of "readiness to buy" as a person walking into a brokerage office, but no one said it did. They are most certainly vastly different in quality and also vastly different in quantity. And although conversation rates are lower, the transactions are just as real. The numbers that are reaching out online are off the chart and bigger than any other marketing strategy real estate has ever seen.

And we're not just referring to the eyeballs they've been able to attract or the large number of listings they have aggregated. They now have another sensation to deal with in that many tens of thousands of agents have agreed to subscribe to a monthly service that forwards the agent consumer leads for the zip codes they subscribed to. The leads come from the tens millions of monthly web and mobile visitors requesting more information.

By the end of 2013 the largest of these portals—Zillow—had announced some 50,000 agents subscribing to this "new" lead gen service, with agents paying approximately $250 per month… amazing, but that is a different discussion. These agents were amassed in two years and reflect the members of just one of the four primary portals. Should this trend continue, and most of the other portals follow a similar strategy (Trulia already boasts a similar number of subscribers), we could see 200,000 agents using this type of lead gen service in the not too distant future.

The question is not whether you approve or agree with the trend, the strategy, or the exact number. Ask youserlf hower the following question.

QUESTION

Within three three to five years portals are expected to be providing some 200,000 agents with the lion's share of their business through high tech online lead generation. How will this big data play, in your opinion, impact real estate brokerage companies and/or agents in general.

BRIANBoreo

Co-founder & Partner - 1000watt Consulting

who do not prepare.

What often gets overlooked in debates about portals and leads is that for many brokers, leads aren't only a source of business, they are a business. If agents can get more leads more cheaply from a portal than they can from their broker then brokers need to replace that revenue, and that element of value. Which, of course, is far easier said than done, but if I'm a broker looking ahead there are things I need to start doing now to make that happen.

First (this is really a big broker option only), take a proactive stance relative to portals. For most brokers, Zillow and Trulia feel like phenomena that have simply happened to them. Since brokers created and still sustain the portals; surely there is still time to bend them to their purposes. I have seen aggressive and constructive engagement work more often than not.

First of all, I believe most good agents will continue to derive most of their business the way they do now; by referral.

Their capacity to generate business has little to do with portals or technology, at least directly. Online leads have always been, and for the most part remain, the snack food of the middling agent—the person with enough money to pay for them, but not established or skilled enough to rely on his or her own efforts for business. It's this Big Middle of agents, however, that many brokers depend on. So, to the extent that these agents look to portals rather than their broker for business, yes, there will be an impact, and it will generally be good for agents but bad for brokers

Second, start thinking and acting now on a value proposition that still depends less on delivering leads. This is difficult but it can be done. It means not letting tech vendors define the boundaries of what is important and possible for your business and thinking strategically about those problems you are best prepared to solve for the customer: the agent.

Online leads are the snack food of the middling agent.

TAMIBonnell

CEO - EXIT Realty

In order to succeed in any business you have to find a need you can fill better than anyone one else. When the real estate community did not provide the information the public wanted, companies like Zillow and Trulia that were born from other industries, rose to the occasion. Like it or not, in order to effectively provide a service, the real estate industry has to be where the consumer is. Starting with this shift, the trend continued to lead generation and now there are lead routing and tracking companies taking off because of another need not being filled by real estate insiders.

The needs of brands, brokers, agents, and the consumer are changing rapidly. Technology, specifically the speed and quantity of information, is having the biggest impact. Big Data gives us the "what;" our job in all categories is to be better at the "how" and "why." But the fear involved in managing, interpreting, and disseminating the sheer volume of information will be the biggest obstacle necessary to overcome. Antiquated MLS and traditional real estate as well as supporting industries will have to shift from protecting their own "stuff" to providing dynamic, flexible user experiences to give the consumer value.

I believe brands (regional or national franchises) are in a better position than smaller independents to have the necessary systems in place, including those to generate leads and manage follow up and follow through. It has generally been implementation and accountability that have been the weak points in business, but more so in real estate because of independent contractor status. I see major brands adding more franchises because of the cost and learning curve which can be prohibitive to some independents as many will be challenged by both the technology piece and the aging agent population. They may find they no longer want to compete or go through another learning curve. Our company, for example, has a great system in place for intuitive, single-point-of-entry input to connect from the very beginning and all throughout the process, all in one place. It's new and fluid enough to plug into third-party lead generation companies. Considering the ease of use, the single point of entry, the tracking capabilities, and the agile design big brands like ours are able to provide, I believe it will be difficult for individual agents and brokers to compete on their own. I truly believe single-point data entry will have to become the norm.

Another issue—and history has proven that brands will fail if they're not prepared— is this: a company cannot simply provide lead generation on its own. Agents need to understand the business and the market, so providing education is also key. The technology tells us the "what;" the broker or agent needs to be well trained and experienced enough to understand and deliver to the consumer the "how" and the "why."

Brokerages that are destined to succeed will have systems in place to capture leads, follow up and keep agents accountable. We will see many more café-style offices both for the consumers' and the agents' benefit. Companies will be merging to capitalize on their strengths, even more so in the next handful of years, passing the baton to the next generation. Reviews on line will become the rule instead of the exception. Being mobile will be expected by consumers; being able to provide them with information instantly in the way they choose, or they will go elsewhere. Earning and maintaining consumer

I believe the landscape three to five years from now will show a different industry. Big Data and all it entails will force change and inspire higher standards in service and education. And that's a good thing.

loyalty every year will become more difficult in this instant gratification era.

The agents who excel will specialize, first in communicating "how," "how often," and "why" to the consumer. They will stay ahead of the market in disseminating the fire hose of information for their client. They will have reviews on line and will be completely mobile. It will a priority to bring their A game if they expect commission structures to stay the same. Their systems, technology, and service will need to be as intuitive as possible. Agents will need to display fine-tuned negotiating skills while consumers are emotional about their home, and they need to offer consulting based on circumstances such as dealing with seniors, investors, first time homebuyers, etc. All of this and more will be expected as part of the service.

In summary, I believe the landscape three to five years from now will show a different industry. Big Data and all it entails will force change and inspire higher standards in service and education. And that's a good thing.

JEFFREY Detwiler
President & COO - Long and Foster Companies

In today's tech savvy world, prospective and current homeowners have more access than ever before to market information and, whether they're buying or selling a home, they're likely starting their search online.

The Internet is already a huge lead generator for real estate professionals around the world, and that segment will continue to grow, especially if the market remains as strong as expected. Recognizing the opportunities for business growth, real estate companies like ours will introduce new technologies and mobile applications to simplify the total homeownership experience and gain more leads for our agents.

There's no doubt the increased accessibility and the amount of market and property data has changed (and will continue to change) the role of real estate agents and their brokerage companies. With massive amounts of information now readily available they have become more like trusted advisors to their clients, helping them navigate through this big data. Real estate pros like those at Long & Foster simplify the data for their buyers and sellers so they can make smart decisions about their real estate investments. With a professional agent's guidance, complex market data becomes helpful and actionable information.

While the Internet created a world in which real estate begins online, it hasn't changed the heart of the business. We've all heard the saying, "the more things change, the more they stay the same," and that phrase rings true in many industries, but none more so than real estate. No matter if agents begin the real estate process with their clients online—whether it's through a simple email inquiry or a virtual real-time connection—the key to success has always been personal relationships.

The technology and tools available to Realtors® have changed over the years, but the value of personal relationships has stayed the same. A home is often the largest investment individuals make in their lifetime, so it's not a decision made with just a few clicks of the mouse. At Long & Foster, we recognize that fact, so we've relied on our relationships as well as comprehensive marketing and technology solutions to support our agents and their clients. We'll continue to do so in the years to come, ensuring that our agents have the training to build strong business relationships and use innovative technology solutions. The most successful brokerages leverage technology and develop personal relationships—that's the winning combination for today and tomorrow.

PHILIP White

President & CEO - Sotheby's International Realty Affiliates

In the luxury real estate market, we believe real estate professionals will always play a critical role in the purchase process, even as technology continues to evolve and develop.

A real estate transaction is complex by nature, and requires an expert's analysis. New, emerging technologies will serve to make the world smaller. So it is the responsibility of those in the real estate industry to become experts in how to navigate those waters to best serve the client.

At the Sotheby's International Realty brand, we embrace this new world and are always looking at

ways to make our agents more proficient with the latest technologies. Over time, more and more opportunities will be created in the online arena at the intersection of mobile and social media. Those who can utilize these tools to build their sphere of influence will be the most successful. Technology should be used to help define a market, and real estate professionals need to determine how to capture data and mine it. Following that, they need to be able to communicate with buyers and sellers in ways they will understand.

In the future, those in the real estate industry will need to be able to use technology as a tool to more clearly target prospective buyers for high-end properties. This will require a special skill set and will be vastly different than running a classified ad in the paper and hoping the right person reads it.

The pace of technological evolution will always be accelerating. Real estate portals, responsive web design, native mobile apps, search engine optimization practices, and Social Media platforms will come and go but what will be a constant is the personal connection a real estate professional has with a client. As a recent Imprev survey shows, despite the onslaught of portals and their technology platforms, tried and true real estate sales and marketing practices are the greatest way to generate business.

Technology should be used to sharpen sales and marketing practices and to facilitate communication with a client they are most comfortable but will never replace a smart and connected salesperson. While a real estate professional should be savvy enough to know the latest ways to use technology to promote sales and measure results, they must also be refined enough to know what makes the most sense, no matter what the medium is.

PETEFlint

Co-Founder & CEO - Trulia

We can't paint a picture of the world in 2018, but expert predictions can help us glean some insights into the kind of economic environment we should anticipate. For example, the U.S. population is estimated to reach 335 million and these people will need homes. According to a report released by the Congressional Business Office, the economy is expected to improve over this time period, growing on average 3.6 percent per year from 2015 through 2018. This general lift should make home-ownership realistic for many of those 335 million individuals.

> Data will continue to change the game, but immediate access to insights will make real estate professionals more effective.

If these predictions are accurate, and if history is any indicator of the future, the real estate industry can expect to see significant, continued innovation. As a result, I expect three important trends to define the next five years for real estate brokers and agents.

INSIGHTS, NOT JUST DATA, WILL BE THE LIFEBLOOD OF AGENTS.

Data will continue to change the game, but immediate access to insights will make real estate professionals more effective. Agents can benefit from a number of different insights, such as understanding how to generate valuable interest in their listings or how to stand out from the competition. Online platforms that measure engagement and provide performance metrics deliver these types of insights. Ultimately, agents with more insights will be better positioned to market themselves and their listings and meet growing consumer expectations.

OFF LINE ACTIVITIES WILL CONTINUE TO MOVE ONLINE AND THIS IS ACCELERATING.

This trend is important for brokers and agents, first of all, because it will mean improved ROI tracking from better-targeted marketing.

Another example of this trend will be referrals, which have traditionally been off line; they will become powered by the Internet. LinkedIn provides a great analogy—today job applicants have the opportunity to promote themselves online to anyone who is looking, and recruiters wouldn't dream of interviewing a candidate without first reviewing their LinkedIn profile. In much the same way, each agent will have expanded opportunities to build a strong online presence and a potential client, even if referred off line, won't reach out before doing online research to determine that he or she is the right person for the job.

Brokerage offices will become more focused on building a community and less on traditional workspaces. Brokerages that enable a more mobile workforce will have an advantage because time in the office is less important than engaging clients in the field.

TOOLS ARE CONVERGING AND PLATFORMS WILL BE INTEGRATED.

For brokerages, it's not efficient to have multiple technology vendors. The patchwork of services and technology providers will begin to consolidate into several players offering more complete solutions. But it won't be just about consolidation of service providers, there's a need to provide a more integrated experience for professionals across multiple devices with access to all the same data and insights regardless of where they are.

Insights, not just data, will be the lifeblood of agents.

VICTORLund

Co-Founder & Partner - WAV Group

This is a truly multifaceted question that is built on the supposition that portals will continue to grow at their current pace. Remember that more than 50 percent of real estate agents fail to perform a transaction in a year, making the 200,000 threshold of agents appear very lofty. Hence, I have three perspectives.

1. IF THE TREND CONTINUES, AGENT RESPONSIVENESS MUST IMPROVE—OR NOT!

Today, real estate agents fail to respond to more than half of the leads that they get from online portals. That translates to CRM, Lead Management and other response automation to improve the deficiency.

The portals know this problem and have already set plans in motion to serve the consumer and supply handy tools to the agent. Certainly, the role that MarketLeader CRM plays for Trulia, and for franchisors like Keller Williams and Century 21, emphasizes that "agent responsiveness to online leads" is a big problem. I know from watching the readership habits of more than a million visitors to RE Technology that CRM is going to be the centerpiece of the agent's productivity suite. The challenge will be the ever-fractured strategy of who will supply that CRM solution. Is agent CRM the providence of the agent, broker, franchise, or the MLS? Today, each of these sales channels is in competition with the others but regional differences will allow each channel to prevail more or less.

On top of lead responsiveness, lead quality is another problem. Lead quality is bifurcated into a problem because of the underlying data (listing accuracy) and consumer verification with the result of a lot of leads being simply junk. CoreLogic addressed the issue by pioneering lead scoring for their mortgage clients, which they recently moved onto their AgentAchieve CRM solution (at last glance serving 100,000 agents).

If the trend of portals creating more leads for agents continues, lead scoring will continue along with it. It takes drips and drabs of consumer information like an email address, phone number, or a property address to pull information about the consumer into light: where they live; do they rent or own; their likely mortgage or rental payment; their credit score; property AVM; debt to equity ratio, etc. It doesn't take much to pull a lot of consumer information together and wrap it up in context for an agent. I guarantee you that if an agent gets a lead indicating that the prospective buyer just closed on the sale of a $2.4M home, has great credit, and is inquiring about a $3M home, the agent will respond in minutes. That's the outcome that everyone is fighting to deliver. Or Not!

Portals operate on narrow margins. When Zillow and Trulia run out of IPO cash, they will trim everything to sustain themselves. All of the executives will move on to their next ventures and they will wilt. This has happened in the past and I think that trend will continue and be the fate of many portals. They come and go.

2. BROKERS MAY REACT NEGATIVELY—OR NOT!

The current feeling among many real estate brokers is that portals are undermining the relationship they have with their agents and the control that they have over marketing listings. They are responsible for how the listing is marketed on the Internet and they don't believe that they're being displayed fairly. Unfortunately, as long as agents and sellers make the call, syndication to portals will flourish. However, there is a breaking point and if brokers feel the threat by portals strongly enough they may begin to take actions to balance the scale. In some cases that balancing may result in limiting portal partners, negotiating new terms, truncating fields of data, pulling listings, or any number of creative tactics. In reality, portals play a very significant role in generating business today beyond marketing fluff—Or Not!

Some brokers will undoubtedly embrace portals as their supreme business partners and they may even withdraw from the MLS and simply use the portals for their business. They present fewer rules, fewer expenses, and more consumers. This will be a relatively small and insignificant group, but if they are successful the tactic will attract others.

I wouldn't put a lot of stock

When Zillow and Trulia run out of IPO cash, they will trim everything to sustain themselves.

in this, but keep in mind that Zillow and Trulia are both operating brokerages and can hire agents (as Redfin and ZipRealty have done). Moreover, they already have relationships with agents as advertisers and know their listing counts, their lead response rates, even their consumer rating. They could quickly recruit and retain a group of excellent agents.

3. CONSUMERS MAY REVERSE THE TIDE—OR NOT!

There was once a day when consumers would talk to their agent about marketing their home in the newspaper and marketing it in the MLS followed with REALTOR.com shortly thereafter. Today it is all of the above.

Newspapers protected organized real estate by charging high fees to FSBOs and the MLS helped by requiring a real estate broker license. Craigslist and Zillow have no such requirements and other portals may soon follow that path. The consumer may learn that they can reach a buyer just as effectively as their agent by advertising on portals and skipping the agent commission. If they learn that they can use a title company or a lawyer for all of their closing documents without an agent, more consumers may select to go that route. Organized real estate believes that this is the unthinkable, but I think otherwise. Look beyond the borders of the U.S. and you'll see that consumers can very easily sell property unassisted—Or Not!

Consumers may get tired of inaccurate data, listing fraud, and may begin to see that having the inside of their home all over the internet is an assault to their privacy. Rental property owners learned this long ago and hired property managers. Privately listing a home for sale in the MLS without all of that public exposure may emerge as a premium service that the seller desires. The river of online privacy concern continues to rise with consumers. Someday it may reach its banks.

SPENCER Rascoff
CEO - Zillow

> A real estate transaction ultimately will always remain in the hands of a local real estate professional.

Today, and in the future, real estate brokerages and their individual agents will continue to provide essential and important functions to current and future homebuyers and sellers.

Much as we've learned in other industries, companies like Zillow provide a key way for consumers to connect with local real estate professionals. The accessibility of "big data" allows for consumers to be more engaged in the real estate process and understand the range of possibilities ahead when buying or selling a home.

In addition, those same consumers are now more likely to have narrowed the range of possibilities when looking for a new home, allowing the local agent to be more productive and helpful, versus the days when an agent would often spend weeks taking potential buyers from home to home.

The agent of tomorrow and the agent of today share the important thread of providing local expertise and knowledge for the most important purchase in the typical consumer's lifetime. As technology advances, there will be new and exciting ways to make that process more efficient. But, just as WebMD has not replaced doctors, a real estate transaction ultimately will always remain in the hands of a local real estate pro.

SUMMARY, Opinion and Take Away

The emergence of the real estate portal is no longer a trend. Of course—it's a reality. Zillow, Trulia, and Realtor.com are orders of magnitude larger than just about any existing "industry" company we have ever had, whether franchise or brokerage. So, in order to get contradictory responses, we went across the board to gather commentary from many different vantage points.

Let's start with the part where opposing sides do agree. Sotheby's International Realty CEO, Philip White, says that real estate professionals will always play a critical role. And portal frontrunner Zillow's CEO, Spencer Rascoff basically agrees when he says "Today, and in the future, real estate brokerages and their individual agents will continue to provide essential and important functions to current and future home buyers and sellers."

But as our other discussions, whether on innovation or branding or business models, have shown, the issue isn't whether portals will disintermediate the real estate professional. And the issue isn't whether technology will change "who" and "how" we will have the conversation with the consumer. So what is likely to happen as the portals become even more loved and used by the consumer than they already are?

Brian Boero, partner at 1000watt, comes closest to our thinking when he says.

What often gets overlooked in debates about portals and leads is that for many brokers, leads aren't only a source of business, they are a business. If agents can get more leads more cheaply from a portal than they can from their broker, then brokers need to replace that revenue, and that element of value.

We have illustrated in numerous previous editions of the *Swanepoel TRENDS Report* how the existing real estate brokerage value proposition is under pressure. We think Boero is on point when he says that one of the reasons is that providing leads to agents is a business of the brokerage, and when the price to value ratio of leads favors the portals, agents will go there instead, with attendant loss of value for the brokerage.

This is already happening as the portals already have subscribers numbering in the tens of thousands. What happens if they become the source of online leads for 200,000 plus producing Realtors®? Boero suggests that brokerages need to get to work immediately on new value creation:

Second, start thinking and acting now on a value proposition that still depends less on delivering leads. This is difficult but it can be done. It means not letting tech vendors define the boundaries of what is important and possible for your business and thinking strategically about those problems you are best prepared to solve for the customer: the agent.

The brokers believe that they are best prepared to solve the agent's problems. Jeff Detwiler, CEO of the impressive and hugely successful Long & Foster, writes:

The technology and tools available to Realtors® have changed over the years, but the value of personal relationships has stayed the same. A home is often the largest investment individuals make in their lifetime, so it's not a decision made with just a few clicks of the mouse. At Long & Foster, we recognize that fact, so we've relied on our relationships as well as comprehensive marketing and technology solutions to support our agents and their clients.

He goes on to say that Long & Foster will train agents on building and maintaining those relationships, while providing the technology tools (and presumably, those valuable online leads, although he doesn't say so specifically).

And Tami Bonnell, CEO of EXIT Realty writes:

I believe brands (regional or national franchises) are in a better position than smaller independents to have the necessary systems in place, including those to generate leads and manage follow up and follow through. It has generally been implementation and accountability that have been the weak points in business, but more so in real estate because of independent contractor status. I see major brands adding more franchises because of the cost and learning curve, which can be prohibitive to some independents, as many will be

challenged by both the technology piece and the aging agent population.

The thing is, even if brokerages are best positioned and best prepared to help agents with technology, they are not technology companies themselves. Which leads to counsel from Boero, who advocates proactive, aggressive, and constructive engagement with the portals (especially for large brokerages who have market power), and the following from Victor Lund of the WAV Group:

Some brokers will undoubtedly embrace portals as their supreme business partners and they may even withdraw from the MLS and simply use the portals for their business. They present fewer rules, fewer expenses, and more consumers. This will be a relatively small and insignificant group, but if they are successful the tactic will attract others.

Brokers withdrawing from the MLS completely and using someone like Zillow is almost certainly not a national trend in the next few years, if ever. But we do agree with both Boero and Lund that many brokerages—precisely those described by Bonnell—who find technology and implementation challenging will turn to the portals as their partners. Remember, that was also a recommendation from Inman in Trend Chapter #2 (Changes and Innovations); Partner or Die!

Pete Flint of Trulia says that insight, not data, will be the real value for agents. Understanding how to generate interest in their listings by looking at engagement and performance metrics is one such example. He also foresees that referrals will move online, drawing an analogy between LinkedIn and real estate. It is an ever so gentle reference to controversial online agent ratings programs, like Realtor.com's AgentMatch. But the real prediction he makes is that brokers and agents will move toward an integrated platform:

For brokerages, it's not efficient to have multiple technology vendors. The patchwork of services and technology providers will begin to consolidate into several players offering more complete solutions. But it won't be just about consolidation of service providers, there's a need to provide a more integrated experience for professionals across multiple devices with access to all the same data and insights regardless of where they are.

Even if we ascribe some self-interest to the CEO of the company that just so happened to have acquired MarketLeader this year, there is something to Pete Flint's prediction, especially since he and Trulia are in a position to make their prediction a reality.

One implication of the question is that the portals will continue to grow traffic, grow leads, and grow in importance to brokers and agents. If that does come to pass and current growth trends indicate that there is little reason to think it won't, then the value of "back office" systems will depend heavily on integration with the lead generation systems. An all-in-one ecosystem solution, where Trulia generates the leads, provides marketing insights, manages the leads, helps with conversion, and possibly down the line through close of transactions, could be an extremely attractive proposition for the small independents that EXIT Realty targets.

That's the positive. The possible downside, especially for brokerages, is what Boero is worried about. If Trulia, for example, can provide a single platform fully integrated for real estate professionals from initial lead generation to transaction management, and all that the brokerage does is buy that system for its agents, there will be a loss of value. Does that cut out the middleman? It already has in many other industries. So the loss of value isn't at the agent level, it's at the brokerage level. And that's the rub.

I'm not concerned about the large companies like Long & Foster, they're well run businesses, well capitalized, and have great management. They are able to, and most likely will, build custom solutions that integrate the best of what someone like Trulia or Zillow might offer into what they already provide. It's the mid-sized company that doesn't have similar resources that will find themselves on the endangered species list. More than anything else, that fact alone might drive more consolidation in the brokerage business over the next couple of years (a trend we have covered in detail in many previous Trends editions).

What we believe is that the portals will continue their growth. Over the next few years, brokerages will find their value proposition under even more pressure as the portals essentially take over the lead generation role from them. We will see the emergence of major ecosystem type of platforms of the sort that Move and Trulia both have, as well as the similar but philosophically different approach of Zillow that aims to provide tools for free to sell the leads. This will evolve the real estate operating system in general and will put further pressure on brokerages to create unique, differentiated offerings to agents.

And this isn't just possible, it's more likely probable. Remember, the portals are big, they're public, and they have lots of money and have young, digitally-

> And this isn't just possible, it's more likely probable. Remember, the portals are big, they're public, and they have lots of money and have young, digitally-immersed talent.

immersed talent. As they pursue their vision of building their companies and providing a return on investment for their shareholders, how many pieces of the brokers'/agents' side of the fence will be redefined? I think, it's more than you think.

Generally productive and successful agents will be thrilled but their brokers might be less so. It is time both groups to sit down and rewrite their strategic intent and their business plan.

Do It Yourself Real Estate

The use of the term DIY in the context of the real estate transaction serves to illuminate, not just "For Sale By Owner" (FSBOs) but the potential for unbundling the entire home buying transaction.

Do It Yourself Real Estate

While certain lower economic profiles may be the central focus of today's growing consumer cash consciousness, it isn't the only driving force that may grow this trend. There are consumers who consider independence from institutional norms to be a symbol of successful lives. Self-healing, doing your own taxes, growing your own food and involvement in all aspects of life are positive personal goals for many.

Additionally as the Millennial Generation draws closer to its natural home buying juncture it's obvious that their "first time" will not be as easy as it was for the Civic or Boomer generations. To start with, the opening economic profile for the younger Americans today is not what it was for their predecessors. It's generally believed that the younger generations will have less cash to work with and more challenging financial thresholds to meet. As a result they will be looking for ways to shave costs from their real estate transaction.

At the other end of the spectrum are the Boomers who will be downsizing from large homes to more affordable, "sized right" and accessible housing options. Their primary objective will be to convert as much of their equity into cash as possible. Shaving costs from their real estate transaction may also become increasingly important. So, with those possibilities in mind, here is the question we posed:

QUESTION

With the growing shift toward more consumer influence/participation will we, in the next three to five years, experience the emergence/growth of an agent-enabled, but consumer powered, "Do-It-Yourself" home buying/selling business model that may offer a sliding scale service offering and what, in your opinion, will it look like?

RICK**Davidson**

President & CEO - Century 21 Real Estate

This is not an "either or" scenario. The current real estate business model will continue well into the future. Buying a home is emotional and infrequent, and the single largest investment most people will make in a lifetime.

As such, buyers and sellers will continue to engage with a real estate professional with whom they can establish a relationship based on trust and confidence; someone who will protect their best interests. The real estate agent who understands consumer-centricity, possesses local market knowledge and negotiating skills, can move through the complex transaction skillfully, and help validate a home buyer's and seller's decision will be successful in this business.

That said the proliferation of technology fundamentally alters the way agents generate access to consumers and leverage their value proposition. Mobility and connectedness via multiple social networking channels is at the forefront of the real estate business, affecting brands and pushing agents to a new level of transparency and authenticity. This transformation allows agents to have direct contact with consumers and the ability to not only generate meaningful one-to-one relationships, but also many-to-many within their online spheres of influence. This is terrific news for the agent community, and the real estate industry as a whole.

The consumer getting "what she wants, when she wants it" has been, and will continue to be, standard operating procedure for successful real estate businesses. Agents who refuse to recognize this simple fact will have a harder time generating new business than those who embrace, engage, and connect with today's tech-savvy, mobile real estate consumer.

The beauty of this discussion is that consumers can choose the model that works best for them, and that the industry embraces that choice.

Today, and well into the future, the majority of real estate consumers will recognize that selling or buying a home is a considerable financial transaction and one that requires the care and concern of a professional. They will continue to rely on a value proposition worthy of a primary relationship, where people—not "1's" and "0's" or binary codes—find workable solutions to even the most complex transactions. Others will choose the "do it yourself" mode, and a great many of those come back to the agent after realizing the knowledge, time, and effort necessary to successfully complete a real estate transaction.

BOBHale

President & CEO - Houston Association of REALTORS®

The emotional basis of the DIY movement, whether applied to a product, process or service, is threefold. In some cases it's about "saving money," in others it's about being "hands on," and in still others it's about not liking how a current service is offered and wanting to create a "better experience."

An interesting and relevant example can be found in the transportation sector where individuals have a wide variety of options. Considering options other than public transportation, the first decision is whether or not to rent a car that between rental fees, fuel, and parking has become the most expensive and inconvenient option. The next cheapest option, a shuttle, will require sitting in the back of a crowded van that stops at numerous places before it

gets to your destination. So, many elect to move up one more step and use a taxi, but that first requires finding one, which will likely involve waiting out in the cold in a long line or standing on a street corner, and then sitting in another cramped space with a driver who may or may not be knowledgeable about your destination.

At some point in the last couple of years the combination of these three options finally created a service satisfaction vacuum. As is the nature of a capitalistic and entrepreneurial system, that vacuum was filled by a new high satisfaction option called Über. Über is an iPhone-based transportation service whose business model uses an app to connect you with a driver at the tap of a button. Choice is a beautiful thing and getting a ride that matches your style and budget is an option that is expanding globally. When you click the Über app a map is displayed that shows both your location and that of the closest driver. Your next choice is to determine the type of vehicle you want—from compact to luxury—and the closest driver meeting your specifications has 15 seconds to respond to the "lead." If the closest one doesn't respond by sending the consumer a text indicating that they are on their way, the lead is forwarded to the next closest driver. You can then view a picture of the driver, the make of car, the license number, and the driver's mobile number so you can call and provide your exact location. My experience has been that a Über car arrives within two to four minutes of my request. At the end of the trip the consumer must rate the driver on a one to five scale before the app can be closed. The driver also rates the consumer for the benefit of subsequent drivers.

The Über drivers I've talked to all indicate the following standards are in place:

- Drivers must maintain a $1 million insurance policy.

- Drivers must maintain a 4.6 rating or they are removed from the system.

- Consumers must maintain a 4.0 rating.

- Drivers must dress in a professional manner.

- The car must be clean and well maintained.

- Drivers are independent contractors and may log in and out of the system at their discretion.

And, at least in my experience, all of this is for a service experience that averages $15.

HOW DOES THIS RELATE TO REAL ESTATE?

During the 2013 NAR Annual Meetings, Realogy sponsored a 27-hour software writing competition—RetslyHackathon—that saw 25 software engineering teams compete for a cash prize by designing a winning real estate app for a new real estate related product or service.

As I have been discussing Über and its possible application to our industry for over a year I was not surprised to see that one of the top products was called "Curb Call." Here's how it works. During the day, when agents finds themselves with available time they can choose to set themselves as "Available" in Curb Call, enabling them to receive leads from buyers. When a buyer finds a property they like, they can use Curb Call to engage an agent simply by opening the Curb Call app. The app identifies the buyer's location so they can "check in" at the desired property and request a showing from a nearby agent. Available agents nearest the listing who have set their status to "Available" will get a Buyer Alert with the buyer's name and the listing they want to be shown. The first available agent to claim the lead will get the full contact information and access to a pre-qualification letter that was part of the buyer's Curb Call sign up process.

Once an agent has accepted the lead the buyer receives an alert with the agent's name, contact info, "rating" and picture. Then, after the showing, the buyer will "rate" the agent on knowledge and service level. For the agent's protection, before a buyer can make a Curb Call they must go through an ID verification and upload the prequalification letter.

We obviously have no way of knowing whether or not Curb Call will ever see the light day. What we do know is that more and more industries and professions are being changed by innovation and consumer adoption. Pandora and iTunes changed the way we listen to and buy music; Google's Chromecast and Apple TV have changed the way we access TV entertainment; Netflix and Hulu have lessened the need for cable; Smartphone cameras are replacing digital cameras; Airbnb is effectively competing with hotels; and Legal Zoom, Turbo Tax and Scott Trade are replacing traditional professionals.

Curb Call is just waiting to be developed, but the real issue isn't whether it will be or not. It's whether we as an industry are going to take advantage of the fact that today's consumer wants both technology and a great experience. We're surrounded by examples of innovative ways in which these consumer expectations are being met in other industries, in fact they are already being met in ours by third parties. Will we keep up? The choice is ours.

MATTHEW Shadbolt

Director of Interactive Product and Marketing - Corcoran Group

> Search is painful. Search is boring. Search is inherently filled with experiences customers don't want.

There's no question that the modern customer, irrespective of the industry, is more empowered than ever before. Empowered through search, reviews, and the ability to vote with their attention.

As everyone from local service professionals to global brands struggle in the fight for digital relevance, to what extent does the customer proactively circumvent those established systems of awareness and visibility, entrenched and established through decades of on and offline activity? How much are customers simply willing, and now able, to do it all on their own?

This is no more acute issue within the real estate industry wherein the role of the agent has undergone seismic disintermediation in the digital era. Many have moved with the customer and adapted. Most have not. I believe that, at scale, dissatisfaction with agents who are

unwilling or unable to adapt to the changing behaviors of their customers, is fueling a move towards a self-service model that further devalues the role of even the best agents.

A clear example of this is the tectonic shift in home search. Once (less than 10 years ago) the listings, the guarded bastion of the agent, are now available for free in hundreds of places online. And the notion of, at least initially, beginning your home search with an agent is now down to single figures within the overall domestic customer demographic. Simply put, customers don't need agents to help with their search, and as they flood into syndication portals that are seeing astronomical growth especially in mobile, they're getting smarter, more educated, and are able to do what even the best agents have prided themselves on in the past.

This behavior shows no sign of slowing down but it's important to remember that customers aren't interested in search. Search is painful. Search is boring. Search is inherently filled with experiences they don't want. What customers are really looking for is finding the right result. This is the insightful, guiding principle that only exists within an agent's head, and is predicated upon listening, understanding, and empathizing.

The right result is always the one the customer wants in a sea of wrong ones. More importantly, it's an incredibly difficult feeling to digitize. While sophisticated levels of tracking using predictive analytics, inferred content, and the sense on the user side that a platform is "learning" the behaviors of its customers, it's still a far cry from the empathetic guidance that only a true human expert can share. Is this a window that's closing within the next five years? Almost certainly, and aggressively so, but as customers gravitate toward excellent services over mediocre, or even great ones, this shift is critical to any industry predicated upon referrals.

What the customer is increasingly willing to pay for is experience, which optimizes their time and actively minimizes search and browsing. Anything that saves time (FreshDirect), excludes advertising (Netflix), or shortcuts decision-making (Foursquare) is becoming highly valuable and sustaining incredible engagement.

Search doesn't optimize time. Find does. And while self-service portals are increasingly prevalent in our lives, from the grocery store to banks, the customer still has to be able to decide upon what to do and how to act. Just because you can cut your own hair doesn't mean you should, or you can, and in an era of deafening online noise, unprecedented choice, and all-time low attention spans, self-service is undoubtedly wonderful.

Want to do it all yourself? Of course you can. But the ability to rise above the chatter and surface the right thing at the right time, for the right person, in the right place, is more powerful. Discovery always wins.

JEFFTurner & BILLLeider

Partners - RealEstateShows.com

While public acceptance of sites like AirBNB have made it ever more obvious that the consumer mindset is primed for a "Do-It-Yourself" home buying/selling business model to emerge, we don't believe we will see anything approaching success on a large scale with this model in the next three to five years.

We continue to hear stories of transactions being done with little or no agent/broker assistance, but those tend to be the simplest and most straightforward transactions. They generally have no issues concerning the property itself, the laws and regulations or title issues, etc. affecting the sale, the disclosure requirements that often lead to lawsuits months after the sale is complete or the

hidden costs associated with the sale. It is well to remember that markets and business models are not built on anecdotes, they're built on large numbers of transactions that contemplate the full range of circumstances that can occur in the sale and purchase of property, the full range of expertise needed to address those circumstances, and the need for people to be protected from their own lack of real estate knowledge.

The simplicity of marketing and finding a home online masks the ultimate complexities of any real estate transaction. Unlike finding a hotel room or trusting a stranger to spend a night in your home, there are a myriad of potential problems that can arise in the progression of the real estate transaction from offer to close that are unique to the personalities, emotional state, and financial status of the parties on both sides of the transaction. They are also specific to the property at the center of the transaction. And while it may be true that the emerging generation of home buyers have grown up in a digital world, once they're involved in the details they quickly come to understand that not all aspects of a transaction can or should be managed without the help of a professional who has navigated the waters in the past.

Instead, we believe they will come to place a premium on the value a truly qualified real estate agent brings to the management of the home buying process. The ability of a broker to provide the resources that enable the individual real estate professional to deliver services at the "financial advisor" level will be key in this environment. Business models don't have to change to make this a reality, but management techniques in the existing business models will need to adapt to insure that the quality of the service provided matches the new elevated expectations of a market that no longer values just access to information.

> Business models don't have to change to make this a reality, but management techniques in the existing business models will need to adapt.

ROBHahn
President - 7DS Associates

At the Hear It Direct event in Orange County in 2013, a group of Millennial elites—doctors, business owners, professionals—said they feel that they already do all the work. In the near future, they said, they would just do it all themselves and not bother with a real estate agent.

I don't see that happening, at least, not in a full-blown DIY model. The real estate transaction remains a low-frequency, high-risk transaction surrounded with quite a lot of red tape. Plus, scheduling showings, getting in to see the property, and managing the transaction from contract to close remain time consuming for the amateur. What I could see, however, is a business model offering fragmented focused service on a pay-go basis. The real estate transaction really has three major parts to it:

- Finding (buyers) and Marketing (sellers)
- Negotiation
- Transaction Management

Quite a few buyers already do most of the work in "finding" the house; a flat-fee "showing agent" service that checks the MLS for the buyer, then opens the door could be a high incremental-margin business. For sellers,

It's just a matter of time.

one could easily imagine a flat-fee service that would do all of the Marketing—input into MLS, syndication to portals, photography, property websites, and schedules showings. Almost all of these are already commodity services that are semi-automated (e.g., syndication, setting up property websites, scheduling showings, etc.)

I can easily imagine an experienced Realtor® agreeing to take $1,000 up front to negotiate the terms of the contract; alternatively, real estate attorneys could do the same on a retainer and write up the contract to boot.

Inexpensive transaction coordinators, many of whom are located overseas, already perform transaction management for real estate agents. Again, a high-margin business opportunity exists to charge an up-front fee to do that work for a client. Charging out a $10/hour transaction coordinator for $25/hour rate is a nice business model.

Put these elements together and you have the basics of an a-la-carte real estate brokerage offering. Obviously, the consumer would save a tremendous amount of money. Less obviously, the model will work because it removes the risk for the real estate agent. In many cases, getting paid out-of-pocket for work performed is a superior business model than hoping that the transaction closes for a percentage of the commission. Driving a picky buyer around to 30-40 houses isn't a big deal if the Realtor® were getting paid $250 per trip.

Will such a service replace the traditional full-service model within the next 3-5 years? I doubt it. But could we see such a service arise? Of course. There's just too much sense in the tradeoff: certainty of income for the professional, and cost savings to the consumer. It's just a matter of time.

SUMMARY, Opinion and Take Away

Do all home buying consumers really still want, or need, to use a real estate professional for all the activities involved in a real estate transaction? Realtors® of course say yes, but that bias aside, is it possible that a substantial group of homebuyers may in the not too distant future prefer to save a huge commission and do some part of the work themselves? If that's the case, could the duties and responsibilities of a real estate professional be unbundled into sub-sets of tasks, priced separately, and therefore offered separately?

Bob Hale, CEO of HAR, acknowledges that the emotional basis of the DIY movement is saving money, being more hands on, disliking the status quo, and wanting something better. He believes that there is such a "service satisfaction vacuum" in real estate today, as there was in transportation, which led to Über, the private taxi service mobile app that is drawing raving reviews from users and defensive moves from existing taxi companies. Houston, for example, is one city where the government will not allow Über to offer its services.

> The company or companies that fill the service gap of offering commodity services at rock-bottom prices will find success.

He goes on to note that similar motivations have led to things like Legal Zoom, Turbo Tax, and ScottTrade, all of which disrupted those service professions. The question then, as framed by Hale, is whether consumers are motivated by the savings, by the hands-on feeling, or by the dissatisfaction with how things are today.

Matthew Shadbolt of Corcoran believes that dissatisfaction is driving the DIY movement in real estate:

I believe that, at scale, dissatisfaction with agents who are unwilling or unable to adapt to the changing behaviors of their customers, is fueling a move towards a self-service model that further devalues the role of even the best agents.

He notes that customers don't need agents to help with their search, and that tools and resources like the major Web portals are helping consumers get smarter, more educated, and do for themselves in a few minutes what even the best Realtors® a decade ago struggled to do. His take, however, is fascinating and it feeds right into one of the themes of this Trends Report—survival of the fittest among agents. But just because consumers have the ability and the tools to do things for themselves doesn't mean they want to. There is no "hands on" satisfaction with buying or selling a home as there might be in building your own deck, or making your own clothes.

The result is that as consumers gain the ability to do more on their own, they will seek our better professionals to provide better experiences:

This behavior shows no sign of slowing down but it's important to remember that customers aren't interested in search. Search is painful. Search is boring. Search is inherently filled with experiences they don't want. What customers are really looking for is finding the right result.

That's just about search, but the idea, we think, applies across the board for the consumer experience of the transaction. Jeff Turner and Bill Leider emphasize this point. Buying or selling a house is quite unlike other DIY projects, even something as "boring" as doing one's taxes with TurboTax:

The simplicity of marketing and finding a home online masks the ultimate complexities of any real estate transaction. Unlike finding a hotel room or trusting a stranger to spend a night in your home, there are a myriad of potential problems that can arise in the progression of the real estate transaction from offer to close that are unique to the personalities, emotional state, and financial status of the parties on both sides of the transaction. They are also specific to the property at the center of the transaction. And while it may be true that the emerging generation of home buyers have grown up in a digital world, once they're involved in the details they quickly come to understand that not all aspects of a transaction can or should be managed without the help of a professional who has navigated the waters in the past.

What they envision instead echoes Shadbolt's insight about more consumer empowerment leads to the need for better professionals. They believe that consumers will come to value the truly qualified agent even more as they gain more and more ability to do things on their own, because doing real estate is filled with pain, risk, and plain old annoyances.

We wanted to also get the opinion of a major real estate franchise and brokerage so we asked, Rick Davidson, CEO of Century 21 one, of the largest franchises in the world. He doesn't think DIY has much of a future in real estate, for all the same reasons as Turner and Leider:

Today, and well into the future, the majority of real estate consumers will recognize that selling or buying a home is a considerable financial transaction and one that requires the care and concern of a professional. They will continue to rely on a value proposition worthy of a primary relationship, where

people—not "1's" and "0's" or binary codes—find workable solutions to even the most complex transactions. Others will choose the "do it yourself" mode, and a great many of those come back to the agent after realizing the knowledge, time, and effort necessary to successfully complete a real estate transaction.

In all of these responses our Thought Leaders agree that more than ever consumers have the wherewithal to do it themselves, but they also believe that the ultimate result will be that they will gravitate toward better agents.

Home surfing on Zillow may be fun but actually buying a home is filled with lots of risk. Consumers may be dissatisfied with how painful the process is, but most of them wouldn't know what to change or how to change it. There is no self-affirming satisfaction with a DIY home sale as there might be with trading stocks and making the right bets.

And yet there is one element that was common with all of the analysis that can change all of that: money. The underlying assumption of all of these answers is that there is no real difference in cost between DIY and using a great Realtor®. But if the examples of Über, AirBnB, TurboTax, LegalZoom, and ScottTrade are any indicators, there is no way that a DIY real estate model wouldn't result in massive cost savings for the consumer. After all, no one uses TurboTax for fun they use it to avoid paying an accountant.

Plus, the question was specific about an "agent-enabled," but "consumer-powered" DIY model. As we noted in Chapter 7, citing Bob Bemis and Curt Beardsley, the technology and much of the process to disaggregate the bundle of real estate services already exists. A precursor to this full "a la carte" model is Jason's House (jasonshouse.com):

A pro at house hunting? Love searching home listings? Why pay an agent to do what you can do yourself? Jason's House puts you in control of what real estate **services** you need and which ones you can pass on. The less you need the more you save.

Jason's House remains a mere forerunner because it doesn't yet break down the entire real estate transaction, like Bemis envisions.

In an age where the "mechanical" aspects of the transaction—filling out forms, coordinating inspections, working with loan officers, dealing with title and escrow, etc.—are carried out not by the real estate agent but by transaction coordinators, title and escrow companies, and even by virtual assistants, we think there is a major disconnect between the price for these mechanical services and their value. Even driving buyers to view homes is often done by licensed showing agents rather than by the "truly qualified real estate agent."

Is there a major opportunity to resell an $8/hr transaction coordinator's services to consumers for $15/hr? Of course there is. If the seller hires a marketing firm to handle all of the photography, online marketing, flyers, and so on for $1,500, would a listing agent agree to cut her commissions by 1 percent? On a $500K house, that's a $5,000 savings to the seller, resulting in a net savings of $3,500. For that matter, couldn't an expert Realtor® who is superbly skilled at negotiation agree to take $1,000 to spend a couple of hours negotiating the deal?

So we actually think it's way too early to discard this trend and believe that as the technology to support an a la carte DIY approach continues to improve, so this model will evolve.

As countless others in the other chapters have stressed time and time again, the smart, tech-savvy, excellent agent with the ability to understand consumer needs, manage communications, and offer a top notch service experience will thrive. And they will do so as the DIY movement grows, because they can and do provide the kind of quality service that matches the consumers' higher expectations. And by delivering not only customer service but customer delight; they will continue to command premium commissions.

But once you exit this top tier of talented agents we believe that the mixed agent-supported and consumer-powered model will be hit with full force. If the quality of service is merely average, and the consumers can do it themselves to save thousands of dollars, they will do so. Not because doing so is personally fulfilling or because they care about the broken status quo, but because they will save a lot of money.

The company or companies that fill the service gap of offering commodity services at rock-bottom prices will find success. They're not competing with the great agent that Corcoran wants to recruit, train, and support. They're competing with the average and below average "mechanical" agents who lack the talent, the expertise, and the experience of the top tier agents.

It seems to us that the Thought Leaders of the industry who contributed to the *Swanepoel TRENDS Report* this year wouldn't mind that so much.

CONSUMER FINANCIAL PROTECTION BUREAU

There are numerous federal and local entities and regulations that shape the residential real estate brokerage business and the home buying transaction, but this one could have the biggest impact we have seen for a long time.

Consumer Financial Protection Bureau

Throughout the history of organized real estate, and despite its key role in the U.S. economy, the marketplace has been largely free from federal regulatory interference (RESPA being a noticeable exception). The Consumer Financial Protection Bureau (CFPB) created in 2011, following the passage of the Dodd–Frank Wall Street Reform and Consumer Protection Act, however is potentially very different.

The CFPB is funded outside the appropriations process by the Federal Reserve, has broad authority and has been given independent agency status. This is not the norm for an independent agency and makes the CFPB now one of the most powerful agencies in Washington. In many respects, some people believe that the CFPB has taken over some of the power from the Treasury and its sub-departments, such as HUD and FHA.

The CFPB's first undertaking in the home buying transaction was to bring some manner of regulatory guidance to the mortgage industry, which it deemed largely responsible for the housing crash that in turn led to the great recession. In doing so the bureau effected almost 1,000 individual regulations to provide consumer protection with regard to financial products and services. Then the CFPB expanded its attention to include complaints dealing with various joint ventures and affiliated businesses within the real estate industry and specifically the relationships between lenders and the third parties (affiliated business arrangements; ABAs).

We think that is close enough to justify asking Thought Leaders:

QUESTION

In what ways and to what extent will the Consumer Financial Protection Bureau (CFPB) and/or other new regulations reshape the real estate business over the next 3-5 years?

MATTHEW Ferrara

Founder & President - Matthew Ferrara and Company

The CFPB and other provisions of the Dodd-Frank Act herald an era of hyper-regulation that will menace the real estate industry and consumers for years.

Like the Credit Card Act (2009) and First Time Buyer Housing Credit (2010), CFPB is another exercise in the "law of unintended consequences" that could significantly decrease mortgage lending and stall the housing recovery.

The qualified mortgage will almost certainly limit credit access to low-income and first-time home buyers (such as high debt college graduates). Small businesses and independent contractors, including Realtors®, with difficult

regulation threatened civil and criminal penalties to bank employees who were mandated to sign affidavits attesting personal knowledge of a property's document history. Fearing the risk, banks severely curtailed foreclosure filings, from 4,700 in September 2011, to a mere 80 the following month. The market effect was a crash in inventory, rapidly rising prices, and a wrong signal to builders to create even more inventory. In short: housing affordability for consumers dropped dramatically.

Government regulation loosened standards for lending in the late 1990s, initiating a housing bubble that eventually destroyed trillions in housing assets a decade later. It's unlikely that this new round of regulations will magically turn out all that much better.

> An era of hyper-regulation will menace the real estate industry and consumers for years.

to document volatile incomes, will face challenges securing credit from lenders charged with documenting a borrower's ability to make monthly payments. Furthermore, provisions allowing borrowers to sue lenders if they decide later their loan is unaffordable will almost certainly increase the cost of borrowing, as lenders price the potential for lawsuits and fines into interest rates.

Other regulations will similarly constrain housing. The 3.8 percent tax on investment income and capital gains embedded in the Affordable Care Act will distort secondary-housing and luxury markets, as high-net-worth individuals re-evaluate their tax implications. In markets where the current recovery has been fueled by luxury- and upper-price brackets, cash investors seeking capital gains may slow demand or seek other markets, such as tax-deferred equity alternatives to real estate.

Less predictable but potentially more damaging are recent state regulations, such as Nevada's AS300 passed in 2011 which effectively froze foreclosures for two years. The

JEREMYConaway

President - RECON Intelligence Services

The real estate industry has been remarkably fortunate with respect to regulation with licensure and RESPA forming the bulk of the industry's regulatory concerns for a number of years. But today there is some thought that this regulatory honeymoon may be coming to an end.

In 2006, following several years of ineffective safeguards and careless lending practice, the industry stumbled into the subprime rate crisis and then proceeded to fall head first into disaster with the foreclosure nightmare that many believe led to the great recession. In response Congress, in 2011, passed legislation seeking to cure the ills that led to the disaster. The Consumer Financial Protection Bureau (CFPB) was established under the Dodd-Frank Act with the objective of creating a single agency at the Federal level that would be responsible for consumer financial protection.

Congress provided the CFPB with an independent agency status that places it among the most powerful agencies in Washington. Even its funding sits outside the appropriations process thus freeing it from the most common of political manipulation. But while many don't believe that the bureau will be a game changer, it needs to be noted that it began operations with extensive power and discretion with a mission to reinvent the way that government regulation works; the ultimate regulator's fantasy, the opportunity to create an all-new system. And its change mandate is about using technology and modern marketing techniques to create a new, more personal and highly efficient kind of government regulation and oversight. This agency is actually going to use Social Media tools and techniques in a regulator context because there is the feeling that the agency can make a real difference in creating the kind of government that the Millennial Generation wants to support.

The Bureau's first assault was, perhaps predictively, the student loan system that has long been criticized for its total lack of effective procedures. Its second was the equally distrusted institution represented by the credit card industry. Both of these industries have felt the power of the Bureau's unique approach to research, investigation, and prosecution. However, it's their current target that makes it a potential threat to the real estate industry.

The residential mortgage industry has been the subject of investigation for the past two years. As 2013 drew to close the Bureau was poised to initiate an intensive regulatory scenario aimed at both the mortgage industry and the RESPA sphere with over 900 new regulations covering virtually the entire mortgage process. It's scheduled to take effect over the next year beginning in early January of 2014. The enormity of this regulatory undertaking in and of its self suggests that there will be complications and unintended consequences that will impact the housing market for an extended period of time.

If the regulatory assault on the mortgage industry isn't enough to capture the attention of the residential real estate industry it might consider paying attention to the impact of the Bureau's current focus on affiliated business arrangements (ABAs). Many brokerages use ABAs to participate in the mortgage marketplace and the failure of these agreements could deny brokerages very profitable mortgage opportunities while at the same time placing them in a regulatory compliance crisis.

The CFPB's investigation of ABAs places it in the brokerage office and that's just one step away from the final point of reckoning. Among the many things that it has learned over the last two years is that every family who lost their home to foreclosure not only had a mortgage broker, they also had a real estate agent acting in the role of a "trusted advisor." From this point it's a very short journey to a possible awakening to the fact that these trusted advisors not only gave advice regarding affordability—making them financial advisors—and the likelihood that the "bubble" would never burst, but at the time they were operating with

absolutely no training, supervision, or oversight. Could the Bureau make a finding that real estate agents were in fact operating as financial advisors without portfolio or proper credentials? This very question is being considered.

Should some combination of the above events come to pass a regulatory firestorm could descend upon the residential real estate industry and its ramifications would be intense and far-reaching. Recall that the banking industry has long been engaged in regulatory compliance so the mechanisms were in place when they were required to comply. The real estate industry, however, has virtually no such cultural or administrative infrastructure. The financial challenges of new supervisory, training and/or compliance programming requirements could be overwhelming.

> It's their current target that makes it a potential threat to the real estate industry.

Moreover, while there has never been a time when such an event would have been easily dealt with by the real estate industry, certainly there have been fewer times when it has been more vulnerable. At the very moment when an entire industry is in the process of shifting both its ownership and relationship focus, the arrival of a regulatory invasion might well create the mother of all challenges… or some really outstanding opportunities.

JIMSherry
President - Innovative Solutions

In 2013 Stewart Title warned that there are hundreds of new regulations from the CFPB going into effect January 1, 2014, which will impose a stringent set of rules on the real estate mortgage business.

The adherence to these newly enacted regulations will severely hamper the mortgage industry in the first quarter of 2014 and have a listing effect on mortgage underwriting. And most importantly, the CFPB is headed directly to the real estate brokerage business.

Many brokers operate mortgage companies within their businesses and many more have an affiliation with a mortgage company. This fact alone will invite investigations into real estate brokerages by CFPB, and once "inside" these businesses, fees and charges of most natures will be scrutinized. The brokerage business has remained relatively free of government intervention (RESPA being the exception), but the CFPB has a broad charter that will allow it to peer into all parts of the real estate transaction to look for irregularities, discrepancies, etc.

CFPB Chief Richard Cordray has revealed the scope of his organization's probes in his microscopic review of automobile financing. Mike Jackson, Chairman of AutoNation Inc., the nation's largest auto dealership group, complained last month that in response to CFPB pressure, lenders sent his group warnings for price discrepancies on car payments of a little as $1 or $2 per month. The thrust of CFPB's probe is based upon uncovering possible discrimination against protected groups (minorities). Another revealing stand is that CFPB believes lenders are responsible to police dealers' financial transactions.

If the CFPB is this critical of auto loans, it would follow that the much larger transaction size of home finance will receive as much or more scrutiny. With the facts stated above, there is a clear indication that the brokerages will be held to new regulations imposed by lenders and likely imposed directly on the brokerage. Any charges to consumers are interpreted by CFPB as falling under their charter to investigate. If it's on the HUD 1, it will be looked at. The Government is indeed coming to Real Estate.

MATT Morris
CEO - Stewart Information Services Corporation

Short term, things are going to get more complicated as there are always rough patches with new regulations. Those pending challenges will cause short term difficulties but will ultimately cause those affected to refine business processes and elevate professionalism within the industry.

For example, the increasing scrutiny of service providers by lenders required by the CFPB—combined with very low tolerances for changes to fees on the loan estimate form—should have brokers closely examining their service providers. With the three-day notification requirement, accurate fee estimates are now of paramount significance to ensure that closings happen on time and funds are released. Over time, this should lead to a flight to quality with brokers gravitating to service providers that develop and maintain the highest standards.

While federal regulations are driving heightened standards for acceptable service providers, some states are pushing further with regulations that drive consumers to select their service providers. This tension will prompt brokers to move into an educational role, providing homebuyers with information about the strength and soundness of options, rather than recommending one provider.

Agents will also need more educational information as the increasing regulation at the federal and state levels will necessitate the capability to explain new forms, disclosures, and rules to clients. This elevates the importance of having a network of subject matter experts to ensure the availability of resources and tools to keep agents and clients informed about regulations and, just as importantly, the transactions themselves. In a day when consumers can electronically track when their pizza delivery comes out of the oven, they won't be satisfied with a home-buying process that keeps many steps a mystery. One of the main goals of the new regulatory

environment is increasing transparency for the consumer, which will be a driver of new innovation.

Perhaps the largest concern is whether or not these regulations make it more difficult for consumers to qualify for loans and what this does to the overall demand for real estate services. Estimates on how many potential homebuyers won't qualify for mortgages under the ability-to-repay/qualified mortgage rule vary greatly. We know some buyers won't qualify, making it important for brokers to know quality lenders who are willing to issue a mortgage to people who may not fall under the rule's umbrella but are still good loan candidates.

In the end, the market will make corrections and the industry will adapt to enhance the home buying experience. Those who are attentive to the changing regulations while delivering value added services to the customer will grow their business. That growth will come at the expense of those that resist change and rest on their previous success. As it says in Ecclesiastes, "there is nothing new under the sun."

BENN&LANIRosales

Partners - AGBeat.com

Many real estate brokerages and agents aren't well versed in what exactly the CFPB is, but it stands to dramatically alter the mortgage industry, and to an extent, the practice of real estate.

Since the inception of the CFPB in 2011, mortgage servicers have been a clear target for reform. The agency is considering a series of new rules that would help protect consumers against "costly surprises" from lenders, requiring servicers issue "more clear" mortgage statements and offer better disclosures about fees or loan interest rate changes. Acting director of the CFPB, Richard Cordray said in a speech, "We want to make sure that at all times consumers know how much they owe, what they are paying, and how their payments are being applied." One rule being considered is a requirement of all mortgage servicers to outline, in monthly statements, terms like a breakdown of mortgage payments of principal, interest, and fees, as well as the itemization of the fees and charges, and warnings of possible late fees.

Yet another rule under consideration regards what the bureau calls "force-placed" insurance, or property insurance the bank takes out for homeowners who miss an insurance payment. Servicers may be required to request proof of insurance before charging for force-placed insurance.

Lastly, another rule could require servicers to explain in better detail how a new interest rate is calculated when it changes, when it will take effect, and issue warnings of future interest rate changes and penalty fees on mortgages paid off early.

What all of this means for real estate brokers is that not only will disclosure forms change, requiring updates across all brokers' systems, these protections seek to make the process more clear, reducing surprises and hopefully, less calls from homeowners down the road who never truly understood the terms of their loan in the first place.

The agency has already introduced new HUD-1 closing disclosure forms to replace existing forms by August 1, 2015. They are designed to make it very easy for any consumer to review and understand, but there are bugs left to be worked out. An example is to include rules associated with the forms such as the three-day rule requiring a final HUD-1 be provided to the borrower a full three days before a closing. But anyone who has ever been at a closing table where changes take place in the eleventh hour knows that requiring a three-day window could delay most closings.

The CFPB seeks to help the consumer, but with their first major announcement they've already unveiled serious problems with implementation. The catch-22 is that while the intention is good, politics often overlooks the little guy (the consumer) and the final outcome of each individual regulation is yet to be seen. There is a very serious danger of over-regulation. Today it's mortgage servicers, but tomorrow it may be mortgage brokers under the microscope, depending on who it's popular to blame for any negativity in the market.

Mortgage brokers should take note that while the CFPB is currently focused squarely on mortgage servicers, as they should be, once the agency feels they have conquered that challenge, they'll move on to others in the chain of command. That means that brokers could be looking at a series of new regulations in the name of consumer protection, implying that they were somehow disserving consumers. The only changes that brokers will really see in the next two to three years are new forms and an easier time dealing with servicers. Brokers can enjoy the quiet time over the next few years but when it's your turn the agency will honor you with a series of new CFPB regulations.

SUMMARY, Opinion and Take Away

Here is the tricky part in managing low-probability, high-risk scenarios. Even though the impact of something like a major hurricane or earthquake is catastrophic, many people simply choose not to insure against such events or take simple precautionary steps. Human beings generally tend to not worry about things they don't think will happen to them. Government regulation appears to be one of these low-probability, high-risk scenarios for real estate, except that it really isn't that low a probability given that real estate is a heavily regulated, licensed industry.

So why did I add this to your trend-watching folder? Here is why.

The CFPB is funded outside the appropriations process by the Federal Reserve, has broad authority and has been given independent agency status. This is not the norm for an independent agency and makes the CFPB now one of the most powerful agencies in Washington. In many respects, some people believe that the CFPB has taken over some of the power from the Treasury and its sub-departments, such as HUD and FHA.

So although we do not exactly know how this impacts real estate yet, the Bureau has, since its inception in 2011, quickly taken a deep dive into approximately one industry every year. The first to be investigated and overhauled was the student loan system, which has long been criticized for its total lack of effective procedures.. Secondly was the equally distrusted institution represented by the credit card industry. But it is the third industry—the mortgage industry—that really got our attention.

Jim Sherry, a long term MLS executive and now industry consultant, says that title and mortgage are headed into a regulatory maelstrom:

In September of this year Stewart Title warned that there are hundreds of new regulations from the CFPB going into effect January 1, 2014, which will impose a stringent set of rules on the real estate mortgage business. The adherence to these newly enacted regulations will severely hamper the mortgage industry in the first quarter of 2014 and have a listing effect on mortgage underwriting.

And he believes that the CFPB, among other regulatory entities, is headed directly to real estate brokerage as well.

Matt Morris, the CEO of Stewart Information Services, writes that even though the regulations thus far are aimed at the mortgage industry, real estate agents and brokers will need to deal with some of the fallout:

Agents will also need more educational information as the increasing regulation at the federal and state levels will necessitate the capability to explain new forms, disclosures, and rules to clients. This elevates the importance of having a network of subject matter experts to ensure the availability of resources and tools to keep agents and clients informed about regulations and, just as importantly, the transactions themselves. In a day when consumers can electronically track when their pizza delivery comes out of the oven, they won't be satisfied with a home-buying process that keeps many steps a mystery. One of the main goals of the new regulatory environment is increasing transparency for the consumer, which will be a driver of new innovation.

If the first three undertakings are anything to go by, real estate most certainly needs to be on heightened alert. The impact may still be a few years away, but we most certainly believe it is coming. So we asked a leading industry consultant, Jeremy Conaway, his thoughts and here what he said:

If the regulatory assault on the mortgage industry isn't enough to capture the attention of the residential real estate industry it might consider paying attention to the impact of the Bureau's current focus on affiliated business arrangements (ABAs). Many brokerages use ABAs to participate in the mortgage marketplace and the failure of these agreements could deny brokerages very profitable mortgage opportunities while at the same time placing them in a regulatory compliance crisis.

The CFPB's investigation of ABAs places it in the brokerage office and that's just one step away from the final point of reckoning. Among the many things that it has learned over

the last two years is that every family who lost their home to foreclosure not only had a mortgage broker, they also had a real estate agent acting in the role of a "trusted advisor."

The resulting "regulatory firestorm" would fundamentally change residential real estate brokerage as we know it. We note that in November the CFPB settled a lawsuit against a Utah mortgage brokerage over bonuses it paid to employees and for failing to keep records as required by LO Compensation Rule. The settlement was for $13 million.

If the CFPB can regulate how loan officers can be paid, and what records brokers are required to keep, it strikes us as not impossible to think that it might take an interest in how real estate agents are paid as well, especially in light of what Conaway mentions above: most of those people who lost their homes to foreclosure had a Realtor® helping them buy that house.

The real estate industry has been remarkably fortunate with respect to regulation with licensure and RESPA forming the bulk of the industry's regulatory concerns for a number of years. But today there is some thought that this regulatory honeymoon may be coming to an end.

And Matthew Ferrara, another industry consultant and trainer, concurs and sums it up nicely when he says, "The CFPB and other provisions of the Dodd-Frank Act herald an era of hyper-regulation that will menace the real estate industry and consumers for years."

Lani Rosales, one part of the husband and wife duo that created *AGBeat*, points out one example involving the new HUD-1 forms:

The agency has already introduced new HUD-1 closing disclosure forms to replace existing forms by August 1, 2015. They are designed to make it very easy for any consumer to review and understand, but there are bugs left to be worked out. An example is to include rules associated with the forms such as the three-day rule requiring a final HUD-1 be provided to the borrower a full three days before a closing. But anyone who has ever been at a closing table where changes take place in the eleventh hour knows that requiring a three-day window could delay most closings.

But before I get completely engrossed in the CFPB, Ferrara reminded us that there are plenty of other governmental entities and regulations for the industry to be concerned about as well, including state regulations:

Less predictable but potentially more damaging are recent state regulations, such as Nevada's AS300 passed in 2011, which effectively froze foreclosures for two years. The regulation threatened civil and criminal penalties to bank employees who were mandated to sign affidavits attesting personal knowledge of a property's document history. Fearing the risk, banks severely curtailed foreclosure filings, from 4,700 in September 2011, to a mere 80 the following

are siblings, so it would be a short skip over to directly regulating brokerage services in the name of consumer protection. The trend towards regulation in the wider housing sector is indisputable. And regulation is one of those low-risk high-impact scenarios before which the real estate industry is helpless. Should the CFPB prohibit the sharing of brokerage commissions, to take one example, it isn't clear that there is anything that any brokerage, no matter how large, could do about it except obey. This isn't like tension with the MLS or Realtor® Associations or squabbling over Zillow or Trulia, this will be different.

It's important to note that we are entering into this environment of heightened regulatory activity at the precise time that: (a) organized real estate, the traditional bulwark of the industry against government action, is itself in transition; (b) a large number of companies have consolidated and the industry is controlled by fewer bigger players that ever before; (c) that we have more public entities with deep pockets that are able to pay fines but

> The mortgage and real estate brokerage industry are siblings, so it would be a short skip over to directly regulating brokerage services in the name of consumer protection.

month. The market effect was a crash in inventory, rapidly rising prices, and a wrong signal to builders to create even more inventory. In short: housing affordability for consumers dropped dramatically.

For the moment the actions of regulators are focused on the mortgage industry, and although they will have an enormous impact on the housing market, many will not directly impact the real estate brokerage industry. Nonetheless, as we said earlier, the tricky part is managing low-probability, high-risk scenarios.

The mortgage and real estate brokerage industry

also affect change; and (d) at a time in which the consumer has elevated home surfing to a national pastime and is increasingly balking at the steep commissions they have to pay.

The authority granted to the CFPB will allow them, in the name of consumer protection, to peer into all parts of the real estate transaction to look for irregularities and discrepancies. And look, we think, they will.

Index

Last	Fisrt	Title	Company	Chp.
Allen	Mark	Chief Executive Officer	10K Research and Marketing	5
Allison	Austin	Co-founder and CEO	Dotloop	7
Beall	Matthew	Co-Founder	Hawaii Life Real Estate Brokers	7
Beardsley	Curt	VP Product Marketing	Move, Inc.	2
Bemis	Bob	Founder	Procuring Cause	4
Bergeron	Russ	Chief Executive Officer	Midwest Real Estate Data	6
Blefari	Gino	President and CEO	Intero Real Estate Services	3
Boero	Brian	Partner	1000watt Consulting	8
Bonnell	Tami	President and CEO	EXIT Realty Corp. International	8
Casey	Helen Hanna	President and CEO	Hanna Holdings	7
Charron	David	CEO and President	MRIS	4
Chris	Sherry	President and CEO	BH&G Real Estate	7
Cohen	Matt	Chief Technology Officer	Clareity Consulting	6
Conaway	Jeremy	President	Recon Intelligence Services	4, 10
Crye	Harold	President and CEO	Crye-Leike Real Estate Services	5
Davidson	Rick	President and CEO	Century 21 Real Estate	9
Detwiler	Jeffery	President and COO	Long & Foster	8
Dewald	Gahlord	Founder	Thoughtfaucet	2
Duffy	Dan	Chief Executive Officer	United Real Estate	3
Ferrara	Matthew	Founder and President	Matthew Ferrara & Company	10
Ferry	Tom	Founder and CEO	YourCoach.com	7
Flint	Pete	Chairman and CEO	Trulia	8
Goldberg	Bob	Senior Vice President	National Association of REALTORS®	5
Hahn	Rob	President	7DS Associates	9
Hale	Bob	Chief Executive Officer	Houston Association of REALTORS®	9
Harrison	Jim	President	MLSListings	6
Huskey	Budge	Chief Executive Officer	Coldwell Banker Real Estate	5
Inman	Brad	Founder and Publisher	INMAN News	2
Keller	Gary	Co-founder and Chairman	Keller Williams Realty Int'l	2

Index

Last	Fisrt	Title	Company	Chp.
Kidd	Michael	Executive Vice President	Orlando Regional REALTOR® Assn.	3
Lee	Earl	Chief Executive Officer	Berkshire Hathaway HomeServices	5
Liniger	Dave	Co-founder and Chairman	RE/MAX	5
Lund	Victor	Partners	WAV Group	8
Matthews	Jerry	Founder	Jerry Matthews Advisor	4
McClure	Michael	Chief Operating Officer	T3 Experts	3
McQueen	Kevin	President	Focus Forward Consulting	4
Merage	Cameron	President and CEO	First Team Real Estate	3
Miller	Jack	Chief Executive Officer	T3 Experts	2
Moline	Bob	President and COO	HomeServices of America	4
Morris	Ian	President and CEO	Market Leader (Trulia)	7
Morris	Matt	Chief Executive Officer	Stewart Title Informational Services	10
O'Connor	Pam	President and CEO	Leading Real Estate Companies	2
Perriello	Alex	President and CEO	Realogy Franchise Group	3
Rascoff	Spencer	Chief Executive Officer	Zillow	8
Riley	Pat	President and COO	Allen Tate Companies	5
Rosales	Benn & Lani	Partners	AG Beat	10
Ross	Bernice	Chief Executive Officer	RealEstateCoach	7
Ross	Dale	President and CEO	REALTOR® Property Resource	6
Samuelson	Errol	President	Move, Inc.	6
Sanford	Glenn	Founder and CEO	eXp Realty	3
Shadbolt	Matthew	Director: Interactive Marketing	Corcoran Group	9
Sherry	Jim	President	Innovative Solutions	10
Stinton	Dale	Chief Executive Officer	National Assn of REALTORS®	4
Swanepoel	Stefan	Editor-in-Chief/Publisher	Swanepoel Trends Report + SP200	1
Turner	Jeff	Partner	RealEstateShows	9
White	Philip	President and CEO	Sotheby's International Realty	8
Willis	Mark	Chief Executive Officer	Keller Williams Realty Int'l	7
Zipf	Bruce	President and CEO	NRT, Inc.	6

THE MOST POWERFUL AND INFLUENTIAL PEOPLE

INTRODUCTION

Power is an elusive concept. Merriam-Webster dictionary defines it as "the ability or right to control people or things." Of course, that raises the question of what is meant by "control."

Control is defined as directing the behavior of, or to cause a person to do what you want. Power can also exist even though it may not be exercised, because simply having power can discourage others from challenging it. So you could just imagine the healthy debate we had as to what criteria should be used in creating a list of the most powerful people. Although we are the leading researchers on real estate trends (25+ publications on trends, including the annual *Swanepoel TRENDS Report*) we still had serious difficulty. So for the *Swanepoel Power 200* (SP200), we defined "Power" simply as "the ability to make things happen".

BENCHMARKS

We decided to create benchmarks and algorithms that take into account the individual's personal influence, his/her tenure in the industry, the office he or she holds, the decision-making power of said office, the financial resources of his or her company or organization, that company or organization's significance and contribution to the industry, the company's geographic reach, and his or her recent activities, growth and potential.

And then the SP200 editorial team debated each person extensively, making adjustments based our multiple decades-long experience and knowledge of the people on the list. We know this is more art than science, despite our hours spent on numbers and computer models, and like art, beauty is in the eye of the beholder. We recognize that long after publication, each of us will have at least a dozen individuals we think should be higher on the list.

REAL ESTATE

Real estate is too broad and includes multiple verticals in would be almost impossible to include all occupations and businesses in real estate. It was therefore decided to more accurate to define it as the "residential real estate industry". The residential real estate is an enormous industry with some $55 billion being earned just in real estate commissions every year. Hence we only included those individuals/companies who generate most of their business or income, in one form or another, from the residential real estate industry.

There was some heated debate on whether we should include companies and individuals in finance and government. Obviously, major mortgage banks like Bank of America and Wells Fargo have incalculable impact on residential real estate, and they do have significant revenue from the sale and purchase of residential properties. They however also have significant other revenue. A similar situation arises with powerful regulators and legislators. Our solution was to acknowledge those individuals under the "Outsiders" category without including them in the overall SP200 ranking.

In Residential Real Estate 2013

CATEGORIES

Power players have been grouped in comparable and like-minded categories. For example we have the CEOs and other senior executives that hold corporate positions in the large national/global franchise and similar networks; the broker/owner and/or senior management of residential real estate brokerage companies; the CEO's, CTOs and other senior executives directly involved in technology or whose company is a service provider that primarily focuses on the home buying and selling process; and so on.

Here are the categories:
- Corporate Real Estate Leaders
- Residential Real Estate Brokers
- Technology Leaders
- Trade Association Executives
- Economists and Advisors
- Educators and Coaches
- Media Executives
- Social Media Networkers,
- And a bonus list of the Powerful Women in our Industry

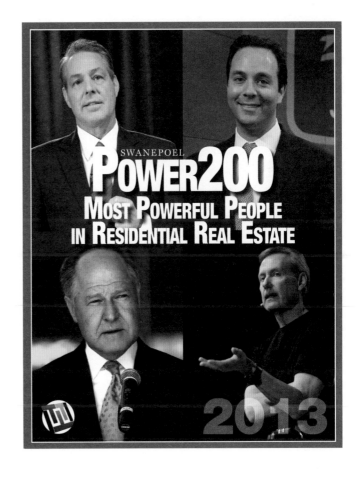

SP200.COM

This is the first issue of the SP200, the most comprehensive analysis ever published of the most powerful key decision makers, trailblazers, influencers, company chieftains, thought leaders, and innovators and you can view the comprehensive list and even download a print friendly 44+ page copy of the SP200.

T3 Experts ™

EXPERTISE ON DEMAND

The practical application of the Trends Report

People keep saying, "Give us an implementable version of the Trends Report." I created T3 Experts to bring the Trends Report to life in your business, each and every month.

- Stefan Swanepoel

Don't Go It Alone

T3 Experts is your strategic partner for understanding and incorporating the significant trends and technologies into your business. No matter what your role in the industry, T3 Experts provides solutions.

Sales Professionals

- Lead Generation Strategies
- Productivity Systems
- Best Practices and Tools

Teams and Managers

- Keeping Agents Current
- Team Productivity Enhancement
- Technology Adoption Programs

Broker and Owners

- Office Optimization
- Trend Forecasting and Preparedness
- Accelerate Decision Making

One Size Does Not Fit All

Understanding who you are as an agent is the beginning of the **T3 Experts** knowledge process. Let us help you navigate the path to maximizing your potential and results.

Real Estate Sales Strategies

Direct Selling

Prospector

Challenges:

- Restricted by time
- Effort dependent
- Lead shortage

Networker

Challenges:

- Restricted by circle of influence
- Difficulty scaling audience
- Confort zone trap

Cold Leads

Warm Leads

Converter

Challenges:

- Hard advertising costs
- Lead conversion challenge
- Dependency & lack of control

Marketer

Challenges:

- Delivering expert knowledge
- Building an audience
- Time & human resource costs

Indirect Selling

Get the full report on the T3 Real Estate Sales Strategies when you sign up for T3 Experts Membership

How We Deliver It To You

Your monthly **T3 Experts Membership** includes:

 Educational Webinars

 Dynamic Q&A Sessions

 T3x3 Interviews

 **Selection and Buying Guides**

 Audio Podcasts

 **Step-By-Step Checklists**

Available 24/7 Anywhere You Are

Your Strategic Partners

Jack Miller
CEO, former CTO of "Most Innovative Brokerage in North America," founder Technology Coaching at Keller Williams Realty.

Michael McClure
COO, creator of Raise the Bar Facebook group and RTB blog talk radio show, co-author Swanepoel Technology Report.

Special Offer to Readers

Become a T3 Experts MBA Member and enjoy the following Limited Time, Special-Offer Bonuses:

- 2013 Swanepoel Technology Report™ [Digital format] - $149 value
- 2013 T3 Summit TED-like Talks [Digital format] - $99 value
- 2014 T3 Experts Technology Buyer's Guide™ - $39 value

Enjoy over $287 in FREE Bonuses by Joining NOW!

Get your membership today at **T3Experts.com/special**